THE
APPLIANCE
COOKBOOK

THE
APPLIANCE
COOKBOOK

Victoria E. Bumagin

Illustrations by Rosalie Schmidt

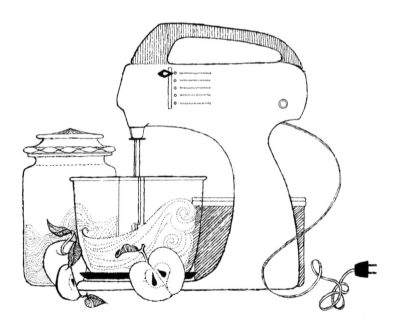

THE MACMILLAN COMPANY, NEW YORK, NEW YORK
COLLIER-MACMILLAN LIMITED, LONDON

The Macmillan Company
866 Third Avenue, New York, N.Y. 10022
Collier-Macmillan Canada Ltd., Toronto, Ontario

Library of Congress Catalog Card Number: 77-132452

First Printing

Printed in the United States of America

Acknowledgments

GOOD COOKING, like good conversation, is a matter of give and take. This cookbook is a collection of recipes—an anthology of pleasant experiences—obtained from, gathered for, and shared with our family and many friends who agree that creativity can be expressed in the kitchen.

For inadvertently laying the foundations of this book, I sincerely thank the many who ate and praised, and the few who will recognize their contributions and influence throughout: Maria Nemetsky, Vera Verosub, Beverly Bramson, Lydia Brown, Emma Hunter, Ruth Karp, Elsie Liebman, and Eve Peterfreund.

To my husband and children, my love and thanks for their enthusiasm, patience, and the spirit of adventure with which they were willing to taste and then to diet. It is with their wholehearted support that this book is dedicated to

ELEANOR PINNER

whom we loved.

Contents

List of Recipes

Preface

COOKING CAN BE a major outlet for creativity available to modern woman.

But take a series of dreary long winter days, with snow and slush in the streets, and the prospect of shopping to cook becomes bleak.

. . . or a heat wave, with appetites lagging and the thought of the kitchen unbearable.

. . . or children sick for a week—mother busy trying to perk up interest and maintain nutrition, worried about the little ones who are bored by having to stay in, while she is running out of food and ideas.

. . . or company coming—what to make is the problem. What did you serve them last? Why not keep a list? After all, how often can you serve chicken breasts in wine?

You face these decisions almost daily, and in each of these situations, whether you thumb through cookbooks or magazines or just rack your brains, you are searching for ideas—WHAT TO COOK?

On the premise that something new usually perks up lagging

interest, how about a new approach to the problem? Why not forget about "what to make"—leave that for last and watch it fall into place—and start with "how to make!"

Look around your kitchen. How many appliances do you have? Are you thinking of them as the helpmates they are? Are you using them to capacity? Do you take them for granted? Are they at your fingertips, always ready to go? Do you discover new ways of utilizing them?

Assume, for example, that you must think of a dinner menu: For the meat course, you decide upon a pot roast, which suggests a fragrant kitchen and conjures the image of a steaming platter of tender slices of meat, covered with savory gravy. "How shall I use my appliances?" Simple! The stove to cook the roast, of course—range or oven, as you will—then the meat slicer or electric knife for the most economical and most attractive serving of it; the food blender for the smoothest, easiest way to make flavorful gravy—and in a fraction of the usual time, three appliances have served you well. But wait—why not also do the roast in your deep fryer, simmering at controlled temperature and keeping the kitchen cool?

You think further: "How shall I make the rest of the meal?" Think again of texture and color and food value. Potatoes? Of course, with that gravy . . . and mashed in the mixer or with a portable beater—is there any other way?

Something crunchy for a side dish—a cranberry and nut mold, perhaps? Where would you be without the refrigerator?

A pack of green beans from the freezer, a fruit pie baked a month ago and frozen, and your dinner is complete. How did you make it so easily? You used seven of the best helpers you could ask for—your electrical appliances!

In this book I hope to help steer you in the direction of using your appliances for maximum efficiency. I think of the kitchen as a laboratory, its modern conveniences as the tools of the trade.

Display them proudly, use them constantly, and be grateful for their help—they can make you a better cook with less effort.

A point of information: In scanning the book, you will find that very often several appliances are required for proper execution of a recipe. Thus, its placement within a chapter is almost arbitrary, and I can only hope that my choice of location agrees with yours. If not, however, the index—arranged by alphabet, not appliance—should overcome our differences. But I have allowed the freezer to cut across the boundary lines simply because it will store almost anything the other appliances help to prepare. Therefore, any food that can be frozen has been marked with an asterisk throughout the book.

One

The Blender

The Blender

O F ALL THE kitchen appliances you own, the blender can be your greatest work- and time-saver and your most exciting partner in innovation. Whenever you need to chop, mix, pulverize, purée, grind, or liquefy ingredients, reach for your blender. With a mere flick of the switch, you will get better and faster results than you've ever achieved before.

The blender offers you a wonderful opportunity to be creative and economical. If you use this amazing appliance to its fullest advantage, you'll find that you can serve a whole array of dishes that seemed impossible or too much trouble to make otherwise. Superb appetizers—from Guacamole to Fish Mousse—can be prepared with ease and assurance. Blender Hollandaise or Béarnaise, made in minutes, can turn a simple meal into company fare. Potato pancakes, which used to be a labor of love, can be a once-a-week treat. Lemon-flavored Veal Rolls, Stuffed Fried Shrimp, and Green Onion Tart are just a few of the dishes you'll be able to prepare with the aid of your blender. And fabulous desserts ranging from Biscuit Tortoni to Rum Chiffon Pie can be created almost instantly.

As far as economy is concerned, the blender can be one of your greatest allies. When you have leftover bits of cheese, don't throw them away. Put them into your blender instead, and make grated cheese for topping casseroles, making soufflés, and flavoring sauces. Or you can buy a large chunk of a cheese, such as Parmesan, blender-grate it, and store it for many months in the refrigerator. Slightly stale bread and rolls should also go into your blender to make bread crumbs for use as toppings, stuffings, puddings, and many other dishes. You'll find that the old problem of what to do with leftovers disappears when you really start to use your blender.

A few simple hints for successful blending: (1) When liquid is called for in a recipe, it is always placed first in the blender, by the dry ingredients. If liquid is hot, blend in very small portions to prevent overflowing. (2) When using dry ingredients (such as nuts), blend only a small quantity at a time; and (3) always use a long-handled, narrow rubber spatula to clear the blades and push the food around for proper blending.

I hope that the recipes given here will introduce you to new adventures in cooking that are as unlimited as your imagination.

NOTE: No time limit in seconds has been set for any blending instructions. I feel it is easier to watch the contents of the blender than the second hand on a clock, and the results are better. You'll have no trouble—the blender will not lead you astray.

Appetizers

BLUE CHEESE DIP

Place in blender container and blend:
3 tablespoons wine vinegar
¼ lb. blue cheese
½ medium onion
1 cup cottage cheese
¼ teaspoon garlic powder
Dash pepper
½ teaspoon salt
Sufficient water (about 2 to 4 tablespoons) to make proper dip consistency, added as necessary.

Cheeses vary in moisture content, so you will have to judge how much water to add once the ingredients are blending. Makes 2 cups.

NOTE: If you omit the water and add instead ½ cup salad oil, you can make a wonderful blue cheese salad dressing. You may also omit the cottage cheese for a thinner dressing, blending the mixture very thoroughly for a creamy white dressing.

GUACAMOLE

Place in blender container and blend:
1 large ripe avocado, peeled and pitted
1 ripe tomato, skinned and cut up
2 teaspoons lemon juice
Dash Tabasco sauce
2 tablespoons mayonnaise
1 teaspoon horseradish

Serve with potato chips or as a cracker spread. Makes 1 cup.

MEXICAN GUACAMOLE

If you like highly seasoned foods, try this version of Guacamole, but go very lightly on the red hot pepper.

In blender, whirl just enough to chop coarsely:
1 avocado, peeled and pitted
1 tomato, skinned and cut up
2 teaspoons lemon juice
1 small sliver canned, red hot pepper

Serve with bland crackers or bread, accompanying other bland spreads. Makes 1 cup.

SHRIMP DIP

Blend together:

1 can frozen cream of shrimp soup, thawed
1 3-oz. package cream cheese
1 small onion, peeled and coarsely blender-chopped
½ lb. cooked shrimp
½ teaspoon salt
Dash pepper

Serve with celery sticks or party rye slices. Makes 2 cups.

CHOPPED CHICKEN LIVERS*

2 hard-boiled eggs, separated
1 medium onion, blender-chopped
4 tablespoons butter or chicken fat, if available
½ lb. chicken livers
¼ teaspooon pepper
½ teaspoon salt
½ teaspoon prepared mustard

Chop egg whites in blender and set aside. Sauté chopped onion in butter or chicken fat until golden. Add livers and cook until browned. Place contents in blender container with pan drippings, add remaining ingredients, and blend briefly on slow speed, just to chop, pushing down with spatula if necessary. Garnish with chopped egg whites. Serve at room temperature. Makes about 2 cups.

TUNA-ONION DIP

Blend together:
1⅔ cups evaporated milk
1 7-oz. can tuna fish
1 package dehydrated onion soup mix
⅓ cup vinegar
1 teaspoon Worcestershire sauce
2 teaspoons curry powder

If thicker consistency is desired, add 2 tablespoons bread crumbs, always on hand because of your blender.

Garnish dip with chopped parsley, prepared by removing stems from parsley and blender-chopping the dry leaves until fine. Be sure to do only a very small quantity at a time, removing chopped leaves from the blender before doing the next batch. Yields 2½ cups of dip.

CARAWAY CHEESE SPREAD*

Combine in blender to make a smooth paste, pushing down if necessary:
¼ cup milk
1 cup cottage cheese
2 teaspoons anchovy paste
½ cup butter, softened
2 teaspoons prepared mustard
1 tablespoon caraway seeds
1 tablespoon capers
1 teaspoon minced onion

Garnish with capers. Serve with crisp crackers. Makes about 2 cups.

ONION-MUENSTER SPREAD

In blender, chop separately, then combine:
¼ lb. Muenster cheese
½ large red onion

Spread on buttered slices of salty cocktail rye bread. Serves 8 to 10.

ANCHOVY SPREAD*

Place in blender container and chop at high speed:
1 small can flat fillets of anchovies, drained
1 small onion

Cream together in a small bowl:
1 3-oz. package cream cheese, softened to room temperature
¼ lb. sweet butter, softened to room temperature
½ teaspoon paprika

Add blended ingredients to cheese-butter mixture. Garnish with paprika. Serve with party breads or crackers. Serves 10 to 12.

MUSHROOM-PAPRIKA HORS D'OEUVRE

16 medium-sized mushrooms
1 small onion
1½ teaspoons paprika
½ teaspoon Worcestershire sauce
2 tablespoons butter
2 tablespoons sharp Cheddar cheese
Salt and pepper to taste
½ cup seasoned bread crumbs (with a blender, you always have these ready)

Remove stems from mushrooms. Sprinkle caps with salt. Place the mushroom stems, onion, and paprika in blender container and chop at slow speed, pushing down as necessary. Add Worcestershire sauce. Sauté this mixture in butter until tender. Meantime, in blender, grate the Cheddar cheese separately, adding it to stem mixture after it has been removed from flame. Season with salt and pepper. Fill mushroom caps with mixture; top with seasoned bread crumbs. Broil about 8 minutes, until lightly browned. Serve hot. Makes 16 hors d'oeuvre.

HOT MUSHROOM CAPS*

2 lbs. whole mushrooms
½ cup bread crumbs
½ teaspoon garlic powder
½ teaspoon salt
A few sprigs of parsley or ½ teaspoon parsley flakes
½ cup Parmesan cheese, blender-grated
¼ cup olive oil

Remove stems from mushrooms. Place mushroom caps in shallow open baking dish, cut side down. In blender, combine mushroom stems with bread crumbs, seasonings, and grated cheese, and flip switch a few times, just to mix. Add enough olive oil to make a paste of the mixture. Pour remaining olive oil over the mushrooms, then sprinkle blended mixture over the mushroom caps. Bake at 350° for 20 minutes, sprinkling with a bit more oil if mixture begins to look dry. Serve hot. This dish may be served as a side dish as well as an appetizer. Serves 6.

NOTE: To freeze, cover pan with foil and store in freezer when cool. To serve, bake unthawed at 350° for 10 minutes, still covered with foil. Uncover, and bake an additional 5 minutes.

ONION-CHEESE PIE*

1 unbaked 9-inch pie shell (see p. 89)
4 oz. Swiss cheese
4 oz. Gruyère cheese
1 tablespoon flour
1 large onion
3 eggs
½ cup light sweet cream
½ cup milk
Salt and pepper to taste
Nutmeg

Individually grate cheeses in blender at slow speed, feeding into machine in small pieces and emptying container frequently to avoid sticking. Toss together gently with flour and place in pie shell. Slice onion into very thin circular slices, and separate layers to make onion rings. Add to cheeses in pie shell. Place in blender container the eggs, cream, milk, salt, and pepper, blend thoroughly, and pour over dry ingredients. Sprinkle with nutmeg. Bake at 400° for 10 to 15 minutes, then at 325° for 40 minutes or until golden. Serve hot. Serves 8 to 10.

NOTE: To freeze, cover with foil and store in freezer when cool. When ready to serve, defrost and bake uncovered at 425° for 5 minutes, then at 325° for 10 minutes more. Or bake frozen pie, uncovered, at 350° for 30 minutes or until golden brown.

ONION-CHEESE HOT CANAPÉS

1 small onion, grated
¾ cup mayonnaise
⅓ cup Parmesan cheese, blender-grated

Grate onion in blender. Combine with other ingredients, mix, and spread on slices of small party rye bread. Broil 6 to 8 minutes, until bubbly. Makes 1 cup of spread.

HOT PASTRY CANAPÉS*

Here is a basic recipe for pastry with which your blender can perform an infinite variety of magic tricks; have your dough ready, and let your blender mix the fillings. You'll find yourself using leftover meats, soups, seafood, sauces, cheeses, cold cuts, or relishes, pickles, and spices, in combinations as varied as the contents of your refrigerator and pantry.

1 8-oz. package cream cheese, room temperature
½ lb. sweet butter, room temperature
3 tablespoons vegetable shortening
3 tablespoons sour cream
½ lb. all-purpose flour

With electric beater, mix cream cheese and butter, shortening, and sour cream. Add flour and mix well. Form into ball, wrap in waxed paper, and chill until firm enough to handle easily. Roll on floured surface, then cut into strips for pinwheel rolls, squares for ravioli-type individual puffs, round cutouts for semicircular filled canapés, etc. This dough freezes beautifully, baked or unbaked, and is thus a most versatile hors d'oeuvre foundation. This makes enough for 36 to 48 canapés.

Here are some fillings—do make up your own, and thank your blender for them!

BOLOGNA FILLING

Enough consommé or milk for easy blending. Salt, pepper, or other seasonings optional.
½ lb. bologna, cut up
1 tablespoon relish
1 tablespoon horseradish
¼ cup mayonnaise

Chop bologna in blender, uncover while continuing to run motor, and then add liquid and other ingredients to form paste. Fill pastry, and bake on ungreased cookie sheet at 350° for 20 to 30 minutes, until golden brown. Serve hot.

MEAT FILLING

Blend together:
1 cup cooked meat
1 slice onion
Gravy or broth for thinning
1 egg
Sprinkling of thyme, salt, pepper, your choice of seasonings (don't overlook ketchup, mustard, etc., and don't be afraid to taste!)

For pinwheel roll-ups, roll dough about ½ inch thick and 6 inches wide. Spread filling on pastry, then roll meat and dough as a jelly roll. Slice roll into 1-inch pieces. Bake on ungreased cookie sheet at 350° for about 20 minutes. Serve hot.

CHEESE FILLING

Place in blender container and grate:
½ lb. Swiss cheese

Combine this with:
1 tablespoon flour
1 egg
Enough milk to moisten for easy handling (mixture should stick together)

Fill squares of dough and circles of dough (cut with a large glass) with mixture, fold in half, and fasten by pressing edges together with fork tines. Bake on ungreased cookie sheet at 350° for 20 to 30 minutes, until golden brown.

PARSLEY-GARLIC APPETIZER

¾ cup water
2 cups fresh parsley
Freshly ground black pepper
3 tablespoons olive oil
1 small can of flat anchovies
2 tablespoons wine vinegar
3 tablespoons capers
3 cloves garlic

Place water in blender. Wash parsley thoroughly, tear into small pieces, and discard stems. Add parsley to water in small quantities, chop, remove into strainer, and continue, reusing strained water until all parsley is chopped. Strain until dry. Drain anchovies, reserving oil. Place in blender and add vinegar, capers, and garlic. Blend well. Remove to bowl. By hand, stir in olive oil, oil from anchovies, parsley, and pepper. Store refrigerated for several hours. Serve cold with crackers as an appetizer, or as a relish with fish or meat. Serves 10–12.

FISH MOUSSE

1 lb. fillet of haddock
½ teaspoon cornstarch
Dash pepper
Dash nutmeg
½ teaspoon salt
2 egg whites
1½ cups milk
½ cup cream

Cut fish into small pieces. Place fish in blender with all remaining ingredients. Blend until smooth, about 5 minutes. Pour into greased 7 x 9-inch baking dish and bake for 1 hour at 350°, until firm like a dry custard. Cut into cubes, and serve cold with a mixture of mayonnaise and chili sauce. Serves 12.

MAYONNAISE AND SOUR CREAM DIP

1 cup sour cream
3 tablespoons mayonnaise
1 teaspoon garlic powder
1 tablespoon chopped chives
½ cucumber, unpeeled and cut up

Combine all ingredients in blender and blend until cucumber is well chopped. Chill to serve with carrot sticks and celery stalks as a dip. Makes 1½ cups.

Soups, Sauces, and Dressings

LOBSTER BISQUE*

1 large onion
1 clove garlic, minced
1 carrot, sliced
2 tomatoes, cut up
1 rib celery, cut up
2 tablespoons butter
⅓ cup dry white wine
⅓ cup sweet red wine
2 lbs. lobster tails, uncooked
¼ cup uncooked rice
1 teaspoon salt
¼ teaspoon pepper
½ pint light cream
1 teaspoon lemon juice

Sauté onion, garlic, carrot, tomatoes, and celery in butter in large kettle. When onions are clear, add 1 quart water and wines, and bring to a boil. Poach lobster in this over very low heat, about 30 minutes. Remove lobster, and add rice, salt, and pepper. Continue to boil, covered. When rice is soft, purée soup and three-fourths of the lobster meat in blender, thinning to desired consistency with cream. Add lemon juice. Cut remaining lobster meat into coarse pieces and add to soup, stirring until pieces are well distributed and soup is very smooth. Serves 6 to 8.

STRACCIATELLA (SPINACH SOUP)*

1½ quarts highly salted and peppered chicken broth (canned may be used)
1 package frozen chopped spinach
4 eggs
3 tablespoons flour
3 tablespoons Parmesan cheese, blender-grated
2 tablespoons lemon juice

Bring 4 cups of broth to a boil (set 2 cups aside, for later use), add the frozen spinach, and cook according to directions on package. In blender, beat eggs well, add flour and cheese, and the 2 cups of cold broth. Add this to hot spinach soup in the pot, stirring rapidly until well blended. Simmer over very low heat another 10 minutes without boiling. Stir in lemon juice. Serves 6.

FRUIT SOUP*

3 cups assorted fruit, fresh or dried (peaches, plums, apricots, berries, or cherries)
5 cups water
4 to 6 tablespoons sugar (to taste, depending on fruit used)
1 tablespoon lemon juice
2 tablespoons cornstarch
2 tablespoons water
½ cup sour cream

If using dried fruit, soak overnight, then proceed as for fresh fruit. Combine pitted fruit with water, sugar, and lemon juice in large kettle and bring to a boil. Simmer over low heat, covered, until fruit is very soft (about 20 to 30 minutes). Purée in blender, return to pot, add cornstarch dissolved in 2 tablespoons cold water, and cook to boiling point, stirring constantly. Continue cooking over very low heat another 15 minutes. Serve ice cold, with tablespoon of sour cream in each portion. Serves 8.

VICHYSSOISE*

4 large leeks, white part only, sliced
1 small onion, blender-chopped
2 tablespoons butter
4 large potatoes, sliced
1 quart highly salted and peppered chicken broth
½ teaspoon onion powder
2 cups milk
2 cups light cream
¼ cup chopped chives

Sauté sliced leeks and onion in butter until limp. Add sliced potatoes, broth, and onion powder, and boil gently until potatoes are
done. Pour into blender and blend soup until very smooth. Return
to pot, add milk and cream, and heat to boiling point only. Chill
to serve, adding chopped chives when soup is cold. Serves 8 to 10.

NOTE: This soup is also delicious hot. However, it should never
be boiled after milk and cream have been added or it will curdle.

GAZPACHO

6 ripe tomatoes, unpeeled and quartered
2 large cucumbers, unpeeled and sliced
2 cloves garlic
2 green peppers, seeded and cut up
1 large onion, sliced
½ cup wine vinegar
4 tablespoons olive oil
1 cup chicken broth, cold
1 teaspoon salt
Freshly ground pepper to taste
1 teaspoon basil

Prepare all vegetables. Place some solids with some liquid in blender container and purée. Mixture should not be completely smooth. Transfer to large bowl. Continue this procedure until all ingredients have been puréed—you will need to refill container several times. Taste, adjust seasonings, and chill until ready to serve.

GARNISHES

4 scallions, tips and greens, thinly sliced
1 green pepper, seeded and finely diced
1 large cucumber, unpeeled, seeded, and finely diced
3 tablespoons butter
¼ teaspoon garlic powder
1 cup bread cubes

Prepare vegetables and refrigerate. Melt butter in skillet, add garlic powder, and brown bread cubes, turning frequently. Add these croutons and the cut vegetables to soup just before serving. Serves 8 to 10.

CREAM OF MUSHROOM SOUP*

2 lbs. mushrooms, sliced
1 small onion, sliced
3 tablespoons butter
1 quart chicken broth
¼ cup flour
1 teaspoon salt
¼ teaspoon pepper
2 cups milk
¼ cup sherry

Brown mushrooms and onion in butter. Transfer in small portions to blender and chop fine, each time using just enough of the broth for easy blending. Add flour and seasonings and mix. Return to pot, add remaining broth, and stir in milk and sherry. Simmer gently until hot, stirring constantly. Serves 8 to 10.

SPLIT PEA SOUP*

2 cups dried split peas
2 quarts boiling water (or broth left over from boiling a ham)
1 ham bone, or 1 ham hock
1 small onion, chopped
2 ribs celery, chopped
1½ cups additional ham broth or, if unavailable, chicken or beef consommé
1 teaspoon salt
¼ teaspoon pepper
2 teaspoons thyme

Wash, drain, then cook peas in 2 quarts water, adding ham bone or ham hock, chopped onion, and celery. Boil for 1½ hours, adding water if necessary. Remove ham bone and set aside. Purée cooked peas in blender, thinning with additional broth. Return to pot with additional liquid and seasoning, and heat. Remove meat from ham bone or hock, dice finely, and add to soup. Serves 6 to 8.

BARBECUE SAUCE*

1 small onion, chopped
2 tablespoons butter
1 6-oz. can tomato paste
1 6-oz. can water
¼ cup cider vinegar
¼ cup unsulphured molasses
1 teaspoon salt
1 teaspoon Worcestershire sauce
½ teaspoon Tabasco sauce

Chop onion in blender, remove, and sauté in butter until limp. Combine remaining ingredients in blender, flipping switch just to mix. Add to sautéed onions and bring to a rolling boil, stirring often. Cook about 10 minutes. Use to baste spareribs or other meats. Makes 2 cups.

BLENDER BÉARNAISE

¼ lb. butter
3 egg yolks
½ teaspoon salt
1 teaspoon tarragon
1 tablespoon chopped onion
2 tablespoons wine vinegar

Heat butter until bubbly. Combine remaining ingredients in blender and blend on low speed for 5 seconds. Turn blender to high speed and pour butter in a steady stream into egg mixture. When thick and yellow, transfer to double boiler and keep hot, but not boiling. Makes 1 cup.

BLENDER HOLLANDAISE

¼ lb. butter
4 egg yolks
1 tablespoon lemon juice
2 tablespoons boiling water
½ teaspoon salt
Dash pepper

Heat butter until bubbly. Put remaining ingredients into blender and blend quickly starting on low speed for 5 seconds. Turn blender to high speed and pour melted butter into egg mixture. When thick and pale yellow, serve immediately or place container in hot water bath to keep hot. Makes 1 cup.

MAYONNAISE

1 egg
1 lemon, squeezed
1 teaspoon prepared mustard
1 teaspoon salt
1½ cups salad oil

Blend together all but ¾ cup of salad oil. When egg mixture is smooth, remove cover, and while continuing to run blender, add remaining oil in steady stream until all oil is used. Makes about 1½ cups.

TARTAR SAUCE

1 dill pickle
1 tablespoon capers
5 scallions
1 hard-boiled egg
1 cup mayonnaise
3 tablespoons lemon juice

Coarsely chop in blender the pickle, capers, and scallions. Add egg and flip switch once or twice, just to combine. Add to mayonnaise. Stir in lemon juice. Chill to serve. Makes about 1½ cups.

COCKTAIL SAUCE FOR SEAFOOD

1 6-oz. can tomato paste
¼ cup wine vinegar
1 cup salad oil
1 teaspoon garlic powder
¼ teaspoon chopped dill
1 teaspoon lemon juice
1 teaspoon ground cloves
1 teaspoon salt
¼ teaspoon pepper

Combine all ingredients by blending. Use to marinate cooked shrimps, crab meat, clams, etc. Makes about 2 cups.

CUCUMBER SAUCE

½ envelope (½ tablespoon) unflavored gelatin
¼ cup cold water
1 cucumber, unpeeled and cut up
½ dill pickle
1 tablespoon capers
6 chives, chopped, or ½ teaspoon freeze-dried chives
1 teaspoon salt
¼ teaspoon pepper
1 cup sour cream
1 teaspoon green food coloring

Dissolve gelatin in water. In blender, chop cucumber, pickle, capers, and chives, and add salt and pepper. Stir in gelatin, then add mixture to sour cream, which has been tinted green with a few drops of food coloring. Serve well chilled with cooked fish or canned salmon. Makes 1½ cups.

SPICY GREEN SAUCE

1 green pepper, cut up
1 small sweet pickle
¼ small onion
Few sprigs parsley
1 teaspoon salt
¼ teaspoon thyme
Dash pepper
¼ cup tarragon vinegar
1 tablespoon salad oil

Put all ingredients in blender and chop. Serve on cooked vegetables, hot or cold. Makes about ¾ cup.

SPAGHETTI SAUCE*

¼ lb. sliced bacon, uncooked
2 large onions
2 carrots
4 ribs celery with tops
2 tablespoons butter
1 lb. ground beef
10 chicken livers
1 6-oz. can tomato paste
6 oz. white wine (measure in tomato paste can)
1 teaspoon salt
½ teaspoon pepper
1 clove garlic
2 cups chicken or beef consommé

In blender, chop bacon, onions, carrots, and celery. Melt butter in skillet, add chopped bacon-vegetable mixture, and sauté until tender. Add ground beef, stirring frequently. When brown, add chicken livers and heat while continuing to stir. Add tomato paste and wine, seasonings, and consommé. Cover and simmer for about 1 hour. Serve with cooked spaghetti. Serves 8 to 10.

FRENCH DRESSING

1 cup salad oil
Juice of 1 lemon
¼ cup wine vinegar
1 teaspoon prepared mustard
1 teaspoon salt
¼ teaspoon pepper
1 clove garlic

Combine in blender, flipping switch only once or twice. Use as is on salads, or add ½ cup Roquefort cheese and use on cottage cheese, greens, or fruit salad containing apples, pears, or citrus fruits. Makes 1½ cups.

COTTAGE CHEESE DRESSING

⅓ sago cheese, pulverized in blender
1 cup cottage cheese
⅓ cup wine vinegar
1 teaspoon salt
¼ teaspoon pepper
¼ teaspoon garlic powder
3 tablespoons sour cream

Mix all ingredients in blender, beginning with sago cheese, then adding remaining ingredients and blending until smooth. Serve on greens or with cold sliced meat. Makes about 1½ cups.

NOTE: Sago cheese, sometimes called geska, is a hard, green cheese made with added herbs on a skimmed milk base. It is usually packed in about a 3-oz. conical shape, and must be grated to be used. Blue cheese may be substituted for sago cheese.

ANCHOVY DRESSING

1 cup salad oil
¼ cup wine vinegar
¼ teaspoon pepper
1 clove garlic
1 green pepper, cut up
2 tomatoes, quartered
1 can anchovy fillets

Combine oil, vinegar, and spices in blender and mix. Add pepper, tomatoes, and anchovies, and run just long enough to chop coarsely. Makes about 2 cups.

MOCHA SAUCE*

1 cup heavy cream
2 tablespoons instant coffee
2 teaspoons confectioners' sugar
1 cup vanilla ice cream, softened
1 teaspoon rum

Mix cream with instant coffee and sugar and whip cream in blender by flipping switch on to high speed and off about 10 times, or until almost stiff. Fold into ice cream to which rum has been added. Chill and store in refrigerator. Use on sponge cake or over puddings. Makes 3 cups.

MARASCHINO SAUCE

1 cup maraschino cherries, drained
¼ cup juice from cherries
1 tablespoon lemon juice
2 tablespoons sugar
1 cup sour cream
1 3-oz. package cream cheese

In blender, finely chop cherries with juices and sugar. Add sour cream and cream cheese, flipping switch on and off just to mix. Serve on fruit salad or gelatin desserts. Makes 2½ cups.

LEMON DESSERT SAUCE

1 package instant lemon pudding
2 tablespoons lemon rind
½ cup lemon juice
½ cup sugar
2 cups milk
2 eggs, separated

Combine pudding, rind, juice, sugar, milk, and egg yolks, and blend until smooth. With electric mixer, beat egg whites until stiff but not dry (egg whites do not stiffen well in blender). Fold into sauce, mixing well. Serve on cakes, ice cream, or fruit. Makes 3 cups.

NESSELRODE SAUCE*

1 cup mixed candied fruit
¼ cup rum
½ cup nuts
½ cup orange juice
½ cup lemon juice
½ cup sugar
1 scant tablespoon cornstarch
3 tablespoons cold water

Soak candied fruit in rum while preparing other ingredients. Chop nuts in blender until fine and set aside. In saucepan, combine juices and sugar, and bring to a boil. Dissolve cornstarch in cold water, add to juices, and stir until thickened. Add nuts and soaked fruits. Chill. Serve on puddings or cake. Makes 2½ cups.

STRAWBERRY SAUCE

1 pint fresh strawberries
1 tablespoon lemon juice
1 tablespoon cornstarch
½ cup water
⅓ cup sugar
1 drop red food coloring (optional)

Blend all ingredients at high speed. Place in small saucepan and cook over low heat, stirring constantly, until thickened. Use hot or cold on puddings, cake, or ice cream.

Main Dishes

CHICKEN CACCIATORE*

1 3 to 3½-lb. frying chicken, cut up
¼ cup olive oil
1 onion
1 green pepper
1 sweet red pepper
1 clove garlic
2 tomatoes
3 oz. canned mushrooms, or 10 fresh mushrooms
1 teaspoon salt
1 tablespoon parsley flakes
Dash pepper
¼ teaspoon oregano
⅛ teaspoon allspice
1 cup tomato juice
1 8-oz. can tomato sauce

Brown chicken pieces in hot olive oil and remove. In blender, chop coarsely on low speed the onion, green pepper, red pepper, and garlic clove. Transfer to pot and then chop tomatoes by flipping switch on and off 2 to 3 times. Combine with other chopped ingredients in pot, add remaining ingredients, and sauté a few minutes. Then add browned chicken, cover, and simmer 35 to 45 minutes. Serve chicken surrounded with cooked spaghetti, spooning sauce over both. Serves 4 to 5.

CHICKEN WITH WILD RICE STUFFING

1 4 to 5-lb. roasting chicken with giblets
1 quart water, with 1 teaspoon salt
1 cup wild rice
1 small onion
3 ribs celery
½ green pepper
Salt and pepper
¼ cup butter

In blender, chop chicken giblets coarsely, then transfer to large saucepan of boiling salted water, reduce heat, and simmer for 15 minutes. Add 1 cup washed and drained wild rice. Cook, covered, until tender—about 30 minutes. Meantime, in blender, chop onion, celery, and green pepper, and sauté this in butter until soft. Add to cooked rice and season to taste with salt and pepper. Stuff chicken with mixture and roast at 350° for 45 to 55 minutes. Serves 4 to 6.

CHICKEN BREASTS IN WINE SAUCE*

6 whole chicken breasts, cut in half and boned
Seasoned salt
½ cup flour
2 tablespoons butter
2 chicken bouillon cubes
1 cup water
¾ cup white wine
1 large onion
1 tomato, peeled
2 cloves garlic

Sprinkle chicken with seasoned salt, dredge in flour, and brown in butter. Remove chicken from pan, add 2 bouillon cubes, water, and wine, and stir with drippings. In blender, mince onion, tomato, and garlic cloves, and add to pan. Simmer a few minutes and adjust seasonings if desired. Arrange chicken in roasting pan, pour gravy over it, and heat at 350° for 45 minutes. Baste continually. Chicken will be moist but not much liquid will remain when it is done. Serves 8 to 10.

TURKEY TETRAZZINI*

2 cups cooked turkey
1 small can pimiento, blender-chopped
8 oz. spaghetti, broken into small pieces
1 4-oz. can sliced mushrooms
1 small onion
1 rib celery
3 tablespoons butter
½ teaspoon salt
¼ teaspoon poultry seasoning
1 can cream of turkey soup
2 cups half-and-half sweet cream
¼ cup Parmesan cheese, blender-grated
½ cup sharp Cheddar cheese, shredded in blender

Cook spaghetti until tender according to package instructions. Drain mushrooms, reserving liquid. Chop onion and celery in blender, and sauté in butter, adding salt and poultry seasoning. Combine soup, cream, and mushroom liquid in blender, mix until smooth. Add to onion sauté and continue cooking gently until thickened. In buttered casserole, combine turkey, spaghetti, mushrooms, pimientoes, and top with sauce, mixing well. Sprinkle with grated cheeses. Bake at 350° about 30 minutes or until golden brown. Serves 8.

DUCKLING WITH ORANGE-RICE STUFFING

4 to 5-lb. ready-to-cook duckling
1 tablespoon salt

Wash duckling and wipe dry. Rub inside cavity with salt. Fill with stuffing and roast uncovered at 350° for 2 to 2½ hours, or until leg can be moved easily and feels tender. Serves 3 to 4.

STUFFING

4 ribs celery
1 orange, with peel, seeded
2 teaspoons honey
1 teaspoon soy sauce
2 cups cooked rice
¼ cup melted shortening
1 egg
½ cup walnuts, in coarse pieces

Combine celery, orange with peel, and honey in blender and chop. Add remaining ingredients and toss together. Makes enough stuffing for one bird.

BEEF STROGANOFF*

2 lbs. tenderloin or boneless sirloin tip, cut into 2-inch strips
1 teaspoon salt
¼ teaspoon paprika
½ cup flour
1 large onion, chopped in blender
3 tablespoons butter
1 cup consommé (powder or cube dissolved in enough hot water to
    equal 1 cup)
½ cup heavy cream
½ teaspoon salt
¼ teaspoon pepper
½ lb. mushrooms, sliced
½ cup sour cream

Combine meat, 1 teaspoon salt, paprika, and flour in paper bag and toss until well coated. In deep kettle, sauté onion in butter until golden and remove to blender. Add consommé, heavy cream, salt, and pepper, and blend until smooth. Place meat in kettle, brown, cover, and simmer for 5 minutes. Add mushrooms and cook another 5 minutes. Add blended consommé-cream mixture and continue to simmer gently another 10 minutes, stirring occasionally. Remove from heat and stir in ½ cup sour cream. Serve with broad noodles. Serves 6 to 8.

NOTE: To freeze, omit sour cream until ready to serve. Add after meat has been reheated and removed from stove burner.

SWISS STEAK*

2 lbs. round steak, 1 inch thick
½ cup flour
2 large onions, blender-chopped
2 tablespoons shortening
1 teaspoon salt
Dash pepper
1 clove garlic
1 stalk celery
½ cup chili sauce
½ cup water
1 small green pepper

Dredge meat with flour and pound in. Sauté onion in shortening in heavy skillet, add meat and brown. Combine remaining ingredients in blender container and chop coarsely. Cover steak with mixture and simmer gently, covered, for about 1½ hours, or until tender. White potatoes, white onions, or carrots may be added 40 minutes before cooking time is up. Serves 4 to 5.

POT ROAST IN GRAVY*

2 onions, blender-chopped
2 tablespoons shortening
4 to 5-lb. boneless beef rump roast
1 teaspoon salt
¼ teaspoon pepper
1 teaspoon oregano
1 clove garlic
1 6-oz. can tomato paste
2 tablespoons flour

Brown onion in shortening in deep kettle, add meat and brown on all sides. Add remaining ingredients except flour, cover tightly, and simmer over very low heat for 3½ to 4 hours, until tender. Remove meat to platter and allow to cool for easier slicing. Add flour to gravy in kettle and heat through. Place gravy in blender, and blend a few seconds, holding cover. This should yield 1½ cups gravy. Serves 8 to 10.

MEAT LOAF*

2½ lbs. ground chuck
1 lb. ground pork and veal, mixed
3 eggs, separated
1 teaspoon salt
¼ teaspoon pepper
4 slices stale white bread
½ cup cold milk
1 tomato
1 carrot
1½ teaspoons parsley flakes, or chopped fresh parsley
1 medium onion
1 clove garlic
6 tablespoons ice water

Mix meat with 3 egg yolks, salt, and pepper. Soak bread in milk until soft, squeeze out, and combine with meat. In blender, combine tomato, carrot, parsley, onion, garlic, and ice water. Blend until smooth and add to meat mixture, distributing it well. Pack into two 9 x 5 x 3-inch loaf pans. In electric mixer, beat egg whites until stiff, but not dry, and spread like icing on top of unbaked meat loaves. Bake at 350° for 1 hour. Cool to remove from pans and slice. Serves 10.

VEAL AND NOODLE CASSEROLE*

8 oz. broad noodles
3 slices stale white bread, blended to bread crumbs and buttered by
   adding 1 tablespoon butter
1 small onion
2 tablespoons butter
2 lbs. veal cutlet, cut into small pieces
1 can cream of mushroom soup
1 pint sour cream
1 green pepper
1 teaspoon salt
1 teaspoon oregano
¼ teaspoon pepper
1 4-oz. can sliced mushrooms, or fresh equivalent
1 cup blender-shredded sharp Cheddar cheese
½ cup blender-grated Parmesan cheese

Boil noodles according to package instructions. Drain, rinse in
cold water, and set aside. Chop onion in blender and sauté in
butter, adding veal to simmer until tender. In blender, combine
cream of mushroom soup, sour cream, green pepper, and seasonings, blending just enough to chop pepper very coarsely. Add to
veal, simmering until heated through. Place alternate layers of
noodles, veal mixture, mushrooms, and cheeses in large casserole.
Top with buttered bread crumbs. Bake at 350° for 45 minutes.
Serves 8.

HOT VITELLO TONNATO*

3 to 3½-lb. rump of veal roast, boned and tied
2 cloves garlic, minced
½ cup olive oil
1 teaspoon salt
¼ teaspoon pepper
1 teaspoon thyme
1 carrot
4 ribs celery with leaves
1 small can flat fillets of anchovy
1 7-oz. can tuna fish
1 cup white wine
1 cup sour cream
3 tablespoons capers
3 tablespoons cornstarch, optional
½ cup cold water, optional

Rub meat with minced garlic and place in large kettle with olive oil, salt, pepper, thyme, carrot, celery, anchovies, tuna fish, and wine. Bring to boil, reduce heat, and simmer, covered, for about 3 hours, or until tender. When done remove meat to cool, and purée ingredients remaining in the pot in blender until smooth. Return to pot and heat through. Remove from heat and stir in sour cream and capers. (If thicker gravy is desired, add 3 tablespoons of cornstarch dissolved in ½ cup of water while blending gravy, then cook until thickened, stirring constantly.) Slice roast, pour some gravy over slices, and serve. Additional gravy may be served separately. Serves 6 to 8.

VEAL ROLLS*

2 cups soft bread crumbs (made from day-old bread)
2 lbs. veal cutlets, pounded thin
1 small onion, cut up
¼ cup butter, melted
½ teaspoon salt
⅛ teaspoon pepper
2 slices cooked sandwich ham, boiled or baked
2 slices Swiss cheese
½ lemon, including rind and pulp
1 rib celery with leaves
1 tablespoon chopped parsley or flakes
3 tablespoons milk
3 tablespoons flour, seasoned with a little salt and pepper
3 tablespoons shortening
1 cup chicken broth

Prepare bread crumbs in blender and set aside. In blender container, combine onion, melted butter, salt, pepper, ham, Swiss cheese, lemon, celery, and parsley. Since ingredients are rather dry, it will be necessary to do this in small portions, emptying container periodically. When completed, combine with bread crumbs and enough milk to hold mixture together. Spread on veal pieces, and roll up, securing with string or toothpicks. Roll in seasoned flour, brown in shortening, add chicken broth, cover, and simmer gently until tender, about 1 hour. Adjust gravy in blender, adding flour and seasonings as desired. Serves 6 to 8.

HASH PATTIES*

2 cups cooked corned beef, beef, ham, or lamb
2 cups cooked potatoes, cold
1 onion, cut up
1 carrot, cut up
1 teaspoon salt
Dash pepper
½ cup liquid (leftover gravy, milk, soup, etc.)
1 egg
2 tablespoons butter

Cut meat and potatoes into small cubes with sharp knife. In blender, combine onion, carrot, seasonings, liquid, and egg. Stir into meat and potato cubes and brown in butter in electric skillet at 375°, turning once, cooking about 10–15 minutes. Serves 3 to 4.

PAELLA

2 frying chickens, cut into small pieces
½ cup flour
1 teaspoon salt
¼ teaspoon pepper
½ teaspoon paprika
½ teaspoon garlic powder
½ cup olive oil
2 cloves garlic, minced
1½ cups uncooked rice
2 cups clam juice
4 tomatoes
2 red sweet peppers
3 dozen hard-shell clams (in the shell)
1 lb. raw shrimp, cleaned and deveined
1 package frozen peas, uncooked

Place flour, salt, pepper, paprika, and garlic powder in brown paper bag and toss chicken pieces until coated. Brown in oil in deep skillet. Remove pieces, add minced garlic and rice to pan, and brown for about 5 minutes, until golden, stirring constantly. Add clam juice. In blender, coarsely chop tomatoes, then add to rice. Simmer gently for 10 minutes. Coarsely chop red peppers in blender, stir into rice mixture, and remove from heat. Place rice mixture and chicken pieces in large casserole. Add well-scrubbed clams in shell, shrimp, and frozen peas. Bake, covered, at 350° for 15 to 20 minutes, or until clam shells are open. Remove cover and bake 15 minutes longer. Serves 6 to 8.

SHRIMP SCAMPI

2 lbs. shrimp, in shell
¼ cup lemon juice
3 cloves garlic
6 sprigs fresh parsley
2 stalks scallions with greens
6 sprigs fresh chives
1 teaspoon salt
¼ teaspoon pepper
1 cup olive oil

Wash and clean shrimp without peeling, cutting partially through back to devein and spread into butterfly effect. In blender, combine remaining ingredients and blend just enough to chop. Pour over shrimp in open shallow baking pan, making sure to coat thoroughly. Cook in hot oven (400°) until shrimp are pink, about 8 minutes. Serves 4 to 6.

STUFFED BAKED FISH

3-lb. fish (whitefish, striped bass, or other white-fleshed fish)
3 eggs
2 tablespoons tomato juice or water
3 cooked shrimp
1 sprig parsley
Salt and pepper to taste
1 bunch scallions
1 cup consommé
½ cup light cream
2 egg yolks

Combine eggs, juice, shrimp, parsley, salt, and pepper in blender and blend very briefly, about 2 seconds. Pour into preheated, buttered pan and make omelet, pushing cooked edges toward center to allow all the liquid to cook. When set, place folded omelet in fish and sew or skewer closed. In blender, coarsely chop scallions and place in pan around fish. Add consommé, and bake at 400° for 35 minutes, basting fish frequently. When done, place cooking juices in blender, add cream and egg yolks, mix, and then cook over low heat, stirring constantly until thickened. Pour over fish to serve. Serves 6 to 8.

GEFÜLLTE FISH*

5 lbs. carp
1½ lbs. yellow pike
1 lb. whitefish
2 medium onions
1½ teaspoons salt
½ teaspoon pepper
Dash sugar
3 eggs, separated
1 cup matzo meal
1½ cups water
3 lbs. carrots
2 lbs. onions
Salt, pepper, dash sugar

Have fish market fillet all the fish, and reserve the heads and bones. In blender, grind fish by flipping switch on and off a few times, doing it in small portions and repeating until all fish is done, adding 2 onions to chop fine as fish is being ground. Combine with salt, pepper, dash of sugar, and 3 egg yolks. Add 1 cup matzo meal soaked in 1½ cups water. Beat this mixture by stirring vigorously and throwing batter by large spoonfuls back into itself, to aerate thoroughly. With electric mixer beat egg whites until stiff and fold in.

In large kettle, bring to a boil 2 quarts of water to which have been added the fish bones and heads, carrots, onions, salt, pepper, and sugar. When at a rolling boil, put in fish balls, which have been rolled into a uniform size, making sure there is enough water to cover. Reduce heat and simmer for 3 hours in covered pot which allows for some of the steam to escape. When done, strain liquid, use some to pour over fish, and cool. Serve cold. Makes about 20 4-inch pieces.

Side Dishes

CARROT PUFF*

4 bunches of carrots, or enough to yield 3 cups grated raw carrots
1 cup matzo cake meal
1 teaspoon salt
1 teaspoon cream of tartar
1 teaspoon baking soda
3 eggs, separated
½ cup brown sugar
½ cup shortening

Grate carrots in blender. Sift together dry ingredients. Beat egg yolks until light, add sugar and shortening, and cream well. Gradually add dry ingredients and mix well. Stir in carrots. Beat egg whites until stiff and fold in. Bake in well-greased mold or tube pan at 350° for 40 minutes. Serves 6 to 8.

POTATO PANCAKES*

2 slices dry white bread
¼ cup water
3 large potatoes, peeled and cubed
1 medium onion, cut up
2 eggs
1 teaspoon salt
⅛ teaspoon pepper

In blender make bread crumbs and reserve. In blender, place water, potato cubes, and onion in small portions, and grate, removing to sieve to drain off liquid, reusing this liquid to grate all potatoes. When done, discard liquid and add eggs, bread crumbs, and seasonings to drained batter. Fry in ½ inch hot fat, dropping 1 tablespoonful mixture per pancake. Pancakes should be turned only once and are done when edges are browned and crisp. Drain on absorbent paper. Serves 4 to 6.

SPAETZLE*

4 eggs
1 cup water
1 teaspoon salt
Pinch nutmeg
Pinch ginger
3 cups flour
½ teaspoon baking powder
3 tablespoons butter

Fill a large kettle with water and bring to a rolling boil. Place eggs and water in blender, cover, and mix at slow speed. Without shutting off motor, remove cover and gradually add seasonings, flour, and baking powder until all is used. Batter will be gummy. Drop by spoonfuls or pour in continuous steady stream into boiling water, cooking 3 to 5 minutes, or until all spaetzle have risen to surface. Drain and rinse in cold water. Butter well, season to taste, adding herbs, poppy seeds, sesame seeds, nuts, or any other flavor you may desire. Reheat in oven in covered dish. Serve with stews and pot roasts. Serves 10 to 12.

GREEN ONION TART*

1 cup prepared biscuit mix
⅓ cup milk
2 cups sliced green onions (about 2 bunches)
1 tablespoon butter
1 8-oz. package cream cheese
1 egg
½ cup milk
½ teaspoon salt
Dash Tabasco sauce

Mix prepared biscuit mix with milk, and pat on bottom and sides of well-greased 8-inch pie pan, fluting rim. Sauté the green onions (bulbs and green stems are used) in butter until wilted and bright green. In blender, beat together cream cheese, egg, milk, salt, and Tabasco. Place onions in pastry shell and pour cheese mixture over. Bake at 350° for 35 minutes, or until knife inserted in center comes out clean. Serves 8.

MASHED BEETS*

6 large beets
½ teaspoon salt
½ sweet red pepper
1½ teaspoons lemon juice
¼ cup sour cream
½ cup buttered bread crumbs

Boil beets until tender. Place in blender and mash, adding salt and pepper, lemon juice, and cream just to combine. Place in buttered baking dish, sprinkle with bread crumbs, and bake at 350° for 20 minutes. Serves 6.

YELLOW SQUASH IN EGG*

2 cups pared, sliced yellow squash
2 tablespoons butter
1 tablespoon vegetable oil
½ teaspoon salt
2 eggs
¼ teaspoon soy sauce
¼ teaspoon garlic salt
¼ teaspoon dry mustard
2 tablespoons dry bread crumbs
½ teaspoon paprika

Slice squash into ¼-inch circles. Melt 1 tablespoon butter in skillet, add oil, and sauté squash until transparent but firm. Sprinkle with salt. In blender, combine eggs, soy sauce, garlic salt, and dry mustard, and beat smooth. Add other tablespoon of butter to skillet and pour in egg mixture, coating all the pieces of squash without breaking. Cook until set and bottom is lightly browned. Sprinkle with bread crumbs and paprika and brown lightly in broiler. Serves 3 to 4.

SPINACH CASSEROLE*

2 lbs. fresh spinach
½ cup light cream
2 tablespoons flour
½ teaspoon salt
⅛ teaspoon pepper
½ lb. mushrooms, sliced
3 tablespoons butter
1 can water chestnuts, sliced
1 cup bread crumbs, blender-made and buttered

Cover washed spinach with boiling water and drain. Chop in blender, adding cream, flour, and seasonings. Sauté mushrooms in butter, then add to spinach. Add water chestnuts. Pour mixture into buttered casserole, top with buttered bread crumbs, and heat at 350° for 10 to 15 minutes. Serves 6 to 8.

AND REMEMBER: Brussels sprouts, cauliflower, broccoli, asparagus, beans—all these are made special with a topping of blender-made Béarnaise, hollandaise, or one of the other blender sauces (See pp. 21–24).

Desserts

BISCUIT TORTONI*

½ cup almond macaroon crumbs (about 10 macaroons)
1 cup heavy sweet cream
2 eggs, separated
⅓ cup sugar
2 tablespoons light rum

Make macaroon crumbs in blender and set aside. Whip cream in blender, by flicking switch on to high and immediately off until cream will stand in peaks—about 10 to 15 on–off flicks. Add half the crumbs to the whipped cream. Remove from blender container. Without rinsing container, place egg yolks, sugar, and rum in it and blend. Return cream mix to blender and combine with other mixture. Remove to a bowl. With electric beater, beat egg whites until stiff. Hold to bowl and fold in. Fill paper baking cups and top with remaining macaroon crumbs. Freeze until firm. Serves 8.

COCONUT-ALMOND ICE CREAM*

½ cup blanched almonds, slivered
½ cup toasted coconut
½ cup sugar
2 tablespoons water
1 cup heavy cream
1 teaspoon almond extract
3 egg yolks
½ teaspoon grated orange rind
Dash salt

Chop almonds and coconut in blender. Transfer to mixing bowl. Combine sugar and water in small saucepan, bring to a boil, and cook 2 minutes. Whip cream in blender by flicking switch on to high speed and off about 12 times, or until stiff. Add cream to almonds and coconut. Without rinsing container, put in almond extract, egg yolks, orange rind, and salt. Combine on high speed, remove cover while continuing to run motor, and pour in hot sugar syrup in slow steady stream. Fold this into cream and nut mixture. Spoon into ice cube trays and freeze 2 to 3 hours. Makes about 1 quart.

SALTINE FLUFF*

18 saltines
4 oz. walnuts
¾ cup sugar
1 teaspoon baking powder
3 egg whites

Break saltines into pieces and place in blender container. Blend to make fine crumbs, then add nuts and chop fine. Add sugar and baking powder and flip switch to mix. Beat egg whites with electric beater. Fold dry ingredients into egg whites lightly until well blended. Bake at 350° in lightly greased loaf pan 8½ x 4½ x 2½ inches for 25 to 30 minutes. Serve warm with ice cream or whipped cream. Serves 6 to 8.

RASPBERRY BAVARIAN CREAM

1 teaspoon lemon extract
1 package frozen raspberries
2 envelopes unflavored gelatin
¼ cup cold water
¼ cup hot water
1 cup heavy cream
3 tablespoons sugar
3 egg whites

Blend lemon extract and raspberries in blender. Soften gelatin in cold water, add hot water to dissolve completely. Add to raspberries and mix. Rinse blender container, then whip cream with sugar by flicking switch on to high speed and off about 12 times or until stiff. Beat egg whites with electric beater until stiff, but not dry. Combine with cream and raspberry mixture. Chill in sherbet glasses until set. Serves 6.

CHOCOLATE CREAM

1 cup heavy cream
1 envelope unflavored gelatin
½ cup milk
½ cup hot black coffee
1 6-oz. package semi-sweet chocolate bits
1 tablespoon sugar
2 egg yolks
7 ice cubes

Whip cream in blender by flicking switch on and off 12 times or until stiff, and transfer to mixing bowl. Without rinsing container, place gelatin and liquids in blender container and blend. Add chocolate bits and sugar, then eggs and ice cubes. Fold into whipped cream and mix. Chill in individual dishes or greased 2-quart mold, until set. Serves 6 to 8.

FROZEN APRICOT CREAM*

1 1-lb. 4-oz. can apricots
1 cup sugar
½ cup water
Juice of 1 lemon (about 2 tablespoons)
Juice of 1 orange (about ⅓ cup)
1 cup heavy cream, whipped

In blender, combine apricots (with syrup), sugar, and water, and blend well. Place in saucepan, bring to a boil, and cook for about 5 minutes. Cool. Add fruit juices and freeze until mushy. Beat well with electric beater, fold in whipped cream, and freeze again, stirring once or twice. Serves 4 to 6.

PECAN PUFFS*

4 oz. pecans
1 cup butter
½ cup sugar
2 cups all-purpose flour
1 tablespoon vanilla
1 cup confectioners' sugar

In blender, chop pecans until very fine. In electric mixer, cream butter and sugar, add flour, pecans, and vanilla. Shape into 1-inch balls and bake on ungreased cookie sheet at 350° for 20 minutes, or until golden. Sift confectioners' sugar over warm cookies, cool, and store in airtight container. Makes about 3 dozen cookies.

RUM BALLS*

30 vanilla wafers (1 cup when crumbed)
1 cup chopped walnuts
1 cup sifted confectioners' sugar
2 tablespoons cocoa
2 tablespoons light corn syrup
½ cup dark rum

Make vanilla wafer crumbs in blender. Transfer to large mixing bowl. Place walnuts in container and chop fine. Add sugar and cocoa and blend to combine. Add this to wafer crumbs. Pour in corn syrup and rum and mix well. Shape into 1-inch balls, which may be rolled in granulated sugar, chopped nuts, or unsweetened cocoa. Store in airtight container. Makes 3 dozen.

NUT TORTE*

8 oz. walnuts
8 oz. blanched almonds
6 eggs, separated
1 lb. dark brown sugar
10 tablespoons flour
2 teaspoons baking powder
1 teaspoon vanilla

In blender, chop finely the walnuts and almonds, mixing both kinds and doing it in small amounts to avoid clogging of blender blades, to yield approximately 4 cups of chopped nuts. Remove. In blender, beat egg yolks with sugar, add flour and baking powder. Beat egg whites with electric mixer, until stiff but not dry. Add nuts to beaten egg whites, folding in gently until well mixed. Combine with yolk mixture, add vanilla, and mix thoroughly. Bake in 10-inch paper-lined spring form at 350° for 50 minutes or until cake tester comes out clean. Serve with whipped cream, if desired. Serves 12.

BASIC BLENDER JELLY ROLL*

4 eggs
1 cup sugar
3 tablespoons salad oil
1 cup Bisquick
2 tablespoons lemon juice
Confectioners' sugar

Combine first 5 ingredients in blender and mix until smooth, stirring down if necessary. Pour into jelly roll pan which has been freely floured and lined with wax paper. Bake at 400° for 10 to 12 minutes. Turn out immediately on towel which has been sprinkled with confectioners' sugar. Remove wax paper. Roll in towel and cool. Unroll to fill, then reroll and ice with your choice of icing, as desired. Serves 8.

Here are several jelly roll fillings:

COFFEE WHIPPED CREAM

1 cup heavy cream
½ cup sifted confectioners' sugar
1 tablespoon instant coffee

Place all ingredients in chilled blender container and flick switch on to high speed and off about 10 times. Remove cover and repeat flicking 2 to 3 or more times, watching to make sure cream stiffens to proper consistency.

PUDDING

Any packaged pudding mix, prepared according to instructions, may be used to fill the jelly roll.

ICE CREAM

When filled with ice cream and iced with meringue and baked in hot oven for a few minutes (until golden), this roll makes an unusual baked Alaska.

PECAN PIE*

1 prepared unbaked pie crust
1½ cups chopped pecans (6 oz. before blending)
5 eggs
1 cup sugar
1½ cups dark corn syrup
½ teaspoon salt
1½ teaspoons vanilla
6 tablespoons melted butter
Whole pecan halves for decoration
1 cup heavy cream, whipped

Prepare pie crust and line 9-inch pie plate. In blender, chop pecans and set aside. Beat eggs and sugar together, add corn syrup, salt, vanilla, chopped pecans, and melted butter, and mix thoroughly.

Pour into unbaked pie shell. Bake until filling is set, about 1¼ hours at 325°. Garnish with pecan halves. Serve slightly warmed or cold, topped with whipped cream. Serves 8 to 10.

LEMON-CHEESE PIE*

CRUST

30 vanilla wafers (1 cup when crumbed)
2 tablespoons butter, melted
1 tablespoon sugar
1 tablespoon lemon juice
Few grains salt

Make wafer crumbs in blender, and mix with remaining ingredients reserving some crumbs for the top of the pie. Press crumb mixture on bottom and sides of 8-inch pie pan and set aside while preparing filling.

FILLING

1 cup lemon juice
12 oz. cream cheese
2 eggs
¾ cup sugar

Combine lemon juice, cheese, eggs, and sugar in blender and mix well. Pour into vanilla wafer crust and bake at 350° for 15 to 20 minutes. Remove from oven and cool 5 minutes. Prepare topping.

TOPPING

1 lemon
1 tablespoon sugar
1 cup sour cream

Remove thinnest possible top layer of lemon peel and grate in blender. Mix lemon peel, sugar, and sour cream and spread over pie. Return pie to oven and bake 10 minutes longer. Cool. Chill at least 5 hours before serving. Decorate with leftover crumb mixture and lemon slices, if desired. Serves 6 to 8.

PASCHA (RUSSIAN CHEESE CONFECTION)

½ cup light rum
½ cup mixed candied fruit
¼ cup blanched almonds
1½ lbs. farmer cheese
3 egg yolks
¼ lb. sweet butter, softened
8 tablespoons sugar
1 teaspoon vanilla
½ pint heavy cream, whipped
Seeds from vanilla bean (optional)

Add rum to candied fruit and set aside.

In blender, chop almonds and remove. Place in blender part of the cheese, egg yolks, and the butter, and blend, emptying container and repeating until all cheese is smooth but not liquefied. Remove cheese from container. Blend to chop coarsely the mixed candied fruit soaked in rum, with sugar and vanilla, just enough so that the pieces of fruit are still distinguishable. Rinse blender container and whip cream by flicking switch on at high speed and off about 10 times, or until stiff. Fold into cheese mixture, add fruit and chopped almonds, and place pascha in cheesecloth, twisting it to close tightly over the ball of cheese mixture. Place in colander or strainer over a bowl to catch drippings, placing a heavy weight on top of pascha to speed the draining process. Drain at least 24 hours, refrigerated. Discard drippings. When drained, place mixture, still in cheesecloth, in clay flowerpot or similar vessel, to mold into serving shape. To serve, turn out of cheesecloth onto a platter and decorate with candied fruit and fresh flowers. Cut into wedges to serve 16 to 18. May be accompanied by servings of thin slices of yeast cake or sponge cake or sweet crackers.

RUM CHIFFON PIE

FILLING

2 eggs, separated
6 tablespoons sugar
2 envelopes unflavored gelatin
½ cup light rum
½ cup hot milk
1 heaping cup crushed ice, prepared in blender
1 cup heavy cream

Prepare graham cracker crust according to directions on p. 57, using blender to make crumbs. Allow to cool. In electric mixer, beat egg whites until stiff; then beat in 2 tablespoons sugar. Set aside. In blender, combine gelatin, rum, hot milk, and blend on high speed until well mixed. Add remaining sugar and egg yolks and blend a few seconds. Add ice and cream and blend again. Pour into beaten egg whites and fold gently until mixed. Pour into pie shell and chill until set. Serves 6 to 8.

GRAHAM CRACKER CRUST

15 graham crackers
1 tablespoon sugar
½ teaspoon cinnamon
¼ cup melted butter

Make cracker crumbs in blender with an on–off flicking action, doing no more than 5 crackers at a time and removing to bowl, repeating until all crackers are crumbed. Add dry ingredients and then butter to bowl, distributing well. Press into pie plate bottom and sides and bake 5 minutes at 350° to set. Cool to use. Makes 1 pie crust.

CHOCOLATE CAKE WITH RUM ICING*

CAKE

¾ cup butter
2 cups sugar
4 eggs
6 oz. chocolate bits
¼ cup hot water
2½ cups cake flour
1 teaspoon baking soda
½ teaspoon salt
1 cup sour cream
1 teaspoon vanilla

Cream butter and sugar in electric mixer, then add the eggs one at a time. In blender, combine chocolate bits and hot water and blend to melt. Add to butter mixture, then sift in flour, soda, and salt, alternating with sour cream to which vanilla has been added. Bake at 325° for 35 to 40 minutes in 9 x 11-inch pan. When cool, remove from pan and cover with icing.

ICING

6 oz. chocolate bits
¼ cup hot water
¼ lb. salted butter, softened
2 tablespoons dark rum
2 egg yolks

In blender, melt chocolate bits with hot water, add butter and rum, then egg yolks, and beat until smooth. Spread on cooled cake. Serves 12.

BANANA CAKE

2½ cups all-purpose flour, sifted
1¼ teaspoons baking powder
1¼ teaspoons baking soda
½ teaspoon salt
3 oz. walnuts
3 ripe bananas, sliced
3 eggs
⅔ cup butter
⅔ cup buttermilk
1⅔ cups sugar
1 teaspoon vanilla

Sift flour with baking powder, baking soda, and salt into mixing bowl. Grate nuts in blender and add to bowl. Blend remaining ingredients (no need to wash container) until smooth. Pour over flour mixture, and mix well. Bake in greased and floured 9 x 13 x 2-inch pan at 350° for 40 to 45 minutes, or until cake tester comes out clean. Serve cut in squares, either plain or topped with whipped cream. Makes 20 to 24 squares.

Two

The Refrigerator

The Refrigerator

In the modern kitchen, the refrigerator is taken so much for granted that only when you think about not having one do you begin to appreciate it. I shudder when I remember the time my refrigerator broke down the day before a big dinner party. Usually, the refrigerator is thought of in terms of storage, but it can also offer you a marvelous opportunity to improve your versatility as a cook.

This chapter contains a wide range of appetizing, easy-to-prepare dishes that could not be made without the refrigerator. Marinated mushrooms and pickled shrimp are good examples. Both require only five minutes cooking time. It's the blending of flavors that results from marinating them in the refrigerator that makes these such successful appetizers. At your next buffet dinner serve Beef in Herb-Wine Gelatin, a delicious dish that is also a great convenience since it's made the day before the party. If you like chocolate mousse, you'll love Chocolate Pavé, a luscious dessert that combines mousse with brandy-flavored ladyfingers.

You'll also find recipes here for icy cold soups, crisp salads, and a variety of other cold dishes. All of these plan-ahead dishes serve to make mealtimes less hectic and more fun.

Appetizers

ANCHOVY ROAST PEPPERS

1 7½-oz. jar roasted sweet peppers, cut in slivers
1 2½-oz. can flat fillets of anchovies, cut in 1-inch pieces
½ teaspoon garlic powder
6 to 8 pitted black olives, quartered

Combine all ingredients, discarding the liquid in which the peppers are packed, but using the oil from the anchovies. Refrigerate at least 2 hours to allow for blending of flavors. Serve with crackers or cocktail bread slices. Makes about 1½ cups.

STUFFED FENNEL

**1 bunch raw fennel (also called finocchio or anise), cleaned and cut
into serving pieces, 3 to 4 per stalk**
½ lb. blue cheese
¼ cup salad oil
5 to 6 tablespoons rye whiskey
Paprika or parsley flakes

Mash cheese with oil and whiskey, and fill cleaned fennel stalks,
garnishing with paprika or parsley flakes. Refrigerate until ready
to serve. Serves 10 to 12.

STUFFED EGGS

1 dozen eggs
1 package chopped frozen spinach, cooked, drained, and cooled
⅓ cup cottage cheese
¼ cup grated Parmesan cheese
Salt and pepper to taste
Pimientos or radishes for garnish

Hard-boil eggs. Cool, peel, and cut in halves.

In a bowl, mix spinach with cheeses and mashed egg yolks, and
fill egg whites, taking care not to cover the white. Garnish with
tiny slivers of pimiento or radish. Refrigerate until ready to serve.
Serves 12.

PICKLED SHRIMP

2½ lbs. raw shrimp
½ cup celery tops
¼ cup mixed pickling spices
3½ teaspoons salt

In a large saucepan, cover shrimp with boiling water. Add celery tops, spices, and salt. Cover and simmer 5 minutes. Drain. Cool with cold water. Peel shrimp, devein, and rinse under cold water. Set aside while preparing remainder of ingredients.

2 cups sliced onion

PICKLING MARINADE

7 or 8 bay leaves
1¼ cups salad oil
¾ cup white vinegar
2½ tablespoons capers and juice
2½ teaspoons celery seed
1½ teaspoons salt
Dash Tabasco sauce

Mix marinade ingredients. Place shrimp and onion in alternate layers in shallow dish. Pour marinade over all. Refrigerate and allow to stand at least 24 hours before serving. Will keep at least a week refrigerated. To serve, drain and serve with the marinated onion rings, offering toothpicks as utensils. Serves 12 to 14.

MARINATED MUSHROOMS

1½ lbs. whole small mushrooms, washed
1 cup olive oil
¼ cup white vinegar
Juice of 1 lemon
1 clove garlic, minced
1 teaspoon thyme
½ teaspoon oregano

Place mushrooms in a large saucepan. Add water to cover, bring to a boil, and boil 5 minutes. Drain, and while still hot, cover with marinade. Refrigerate until cold. Serves 12 to 16.

CELERY ROOT MARINADE

2 medium celery roots
½ cup salad oil
½ cup lemon juice
1 teaspoon salt
1 teaspoon prepared mustard
¼ teaspoon pepper

Boil celery roots until tender. Remove peel and cut into slices. Combine remaining ingredients, mix well and use to marinate celery slices for several hours. Serve cold. Serves 6.

JELLIED LIVER PATÉ

1 lb. chicken livers (or 2 boxes frozen, defrosted)
3 tablespoons butter
½ cup Madeira wine (a brandy or Cointreau may also be used)
8-oz. package cream cheese, softened
1 teaspoon salt
2 1-oz. envelopes gelatin
2 #1-size cans chicken broth

Sauté livers in butter until soft. Mash with wine until very smooth. Add cream cheese and salt, combining thoroughly. Chill in refrigerator for easier handling, while preparing remaining ingredients. Soften 2 packs gelatin in cold water, add enough hot broth to dissolve completely, then combine with remaining broth. Pour a little into oiled mold. Chill until jelled. Place paté rolled into a ball in the middle of mold, pouring rest of broth around it. Chill until very firm. Unmold by turning mold over on a platter and running hot towel around it repeatedly until paté is loosened. Serves 12 to 14, as a spread on crackers.

LAMB RIBLET NIBLETS*

3 lbs. lamb riblets (breast of lamb)
1 5-oz. bottle soy sauce
5 oz. maple syrup
1 cup chicken broth
1 clove garlic, crushed

Have butcher cut sheets of ribs into 2-inch widths, cutting across the bones. Slice down meat between ribs, to obtain small squares of meat each containing a bone. Combine soy sauce, maple syrup, broth, and garlic, and pour over riblets in shallow pan. Marinate in refrigerator for at least 2 hours. Bake 1½ hours at

350°, turning occasionally. Remove ribs from sauce, draining ribs as much as possible. Refrigerate ribs and sauce separately, until fat in the sauce has congealed. Lift off fat and discard. Recombine sauce with ribs, and bake again about 1 hour at 350° to heat and glaze. Serves 12 to 14.

FRESH VEGETABLES WITH GARLIC DIP

3 carrots
1 bunch celery
raw cauliflower florets

DIP

½ pint sour cream
6 tablespoons mayonnaise
1 teaspoon garlic powder
½ teaspoon salt
Dash white pepper

Peel carrots with vegetable peeler and cut into thin lengthwise strips. Roll each strip around finger and fasten with toothpick. Clean celery and cut into serving pieces. Slit each stick 3 or 4 times from end toward middle, about halfway down. Clean and break cauliflower into small florets. Place all vegetables in large container with cold water, making sure they are all submerged. Chill in refrigerator for several hours. Before serving, drain thoroughly and remove toothpicks from carrot curls. Serve with dip prepared by mixing sour cream, mayonnaise, garlic powder, salt, and pepper. Serves 12 to 14.

BEAN SALAD

1 #2 can red kidney beans
1 #2 can cut greens beans
1 #2 can wax beans
1 #2 can small white beans or baby lima beans
1 large onion, finely chopped
4 ribs celery, finely chopped
¼ teaspoon garlic powder
1 cup oil and vinegar salad dressing
½ teaspoon salt
Pepper to taste
1 teaspoon dill weed
1 teaspoon oregano

Drain all the beans, add remaining ingredients, and toss very lightly so as not to break up the beans. Chill very thoroughly, refrigerating at least 4 hours. Serves 20 as appetizer, or 12 as salad.

MIXED VEGETABLE SALAD

2 #2 cans mixed vegetables
4 large sour pickles, cubed
¾ cup mayonnaise
1 cup cubed bologna, roast beef, or any leftover cooked meat
1 #2 can cubed beets (optional)

Drain vegetables and pickles, combine with remaining ingredients, and toss to mix well. Refrigerate at least 4 hours for proper blending of flavors. Serves 20 as appetizer, but may be used as luncheon salad or dinner side dish, serving 12.

NOTE: Addition of beets makes the salad pink and sweetens the taste somewhat.

BEET SALAD

2 #2 cans sliced beets, drained
1 cup white vinegar
2 teaspoons salt
6 tablespoons sugar
1 large sweet onion, sliced into rings

Combine vinegar with salt and sugar, add beets and onions, and refrigerate for at least 6 hours. Serves 8 to 10 as appetizer or salad.

Soups

ICY MUSHROOM-DILL SOUP

1 #1 can cream of mushroom soup, condensed
1 soup can milk
2 to 3 teaspoons chopped fresh dill
2 to 3 tablespoons sour cream

Combine soup and milk in a bowl. Blend together thoroughly. Add dill. Refrigerate at least 4 hours. Serve in chilled bowls garnished with a tablespoon of sour cream in each bowl. Serves 2 to 3.

ICED FRUIT SOUP

1 cup orange juice
¾ cup apricot nectar
4 cloves
1 stick cinnamon
¼ cup sugar
1 tablespoon cornstarch
⅓ cup water
1 cup pineapple juice

Mix orange and apricot juices, add spices, and let stand 2 hours in cool place (not refrigerator). Combine sugar and cornstarch and add cold water. Stir until smooth. Heat pineapple juice in top of double boiler, add cornstarch mixture, and cook, stirring, until sauce is thickened and clear. Add strained fruit juices. Place in refrigerator until very thoroughly chilled. Serves 4 to 6.

COLD CUCUMBER SOUP

2 large cucumbers
2 tablespoons chopped chives
2 teaspoons sugar
1 teaspoon salt
2 teaspoons prepared mustard
½ pint sour cream
1 quart buttermilk

Peel and coarsely chop cucumbers. Add chives, sugar, salt, mustard, and sour cream. Gradually stir in buttermilk. Refrigerate 2 hours. Garnish with chives. Serves 6.

Main Dishes

CHICKEN ALMOND SALAD

3 cups diced cooked chicken, preferably all white meat
1 tablespoon finely chopped onion
1 cup diced celery
⅔ cup mayonnaise
1 teaspoon salt
¼ teaspoon pepper
2 tablespoons vinegar
1 15-oz. can pitted black olives
1 cup roasted almond halves

Combine diced chicken with onion, celery, mayonnaise, seasonings, and vinegar. Toss to mix. Gently toss in olives and almonds. Chill in refrigerator till serving. Serves 8.

COLD ROCK CORNISH HENS

3 rock Cornish game hens
Salt and pepper
9 chicken livers
3 tablespoons butter
6 mushrooms, sliced
¼ cup ham, sliced into strips
¼ cup peanuts, shelled and roasted
½ cup soy sauce
⅓ cup melted butter

Wash game hens, dry, and sprinkle inside and out with salt and pepper. In electric skillet, cook chicken livers in 2 tablespoons of butter until barely done. Remove and chop fine. Add remaining tablespoon of butter in skillet and sauté mushrooms briefly. Combine livers, mushrooms, ham, and nuts, and stuff game hens lightly with mixture. Truss birds, and cook, uncovered, in a preheated oven at 350° for about an hour, basting repeatedly with soy sauce and melted butter combination. Refrigerate when cool, and serve cold to 6.

MARINATED ROAST DUCKLING*

5-lb. duckling
1 teaspoon salt
¼ teaspoon pepper
⅓ cup cider vinegar
1 teaspoon Worcestershire sauce
1 clove garlic, minced
⅓ cup chopped parsley

Clean duck and cut into serving portions. Season with salt and pepper. Mix remaining ingredients and pour over duck. Refrigerate at least overnight. Drain off marinade and reserve. Roast duck at 350° for 1 hour and then drain off fat. Continue roasting, basting with marinade every 5 to 10 minutes, until duck is tender, for about another 1½ hours. Serves 5.

COLD BEEF IN HERB-WINE GELATIN

2 onions, sliced
3 tablespoons butter
5-lb. boneless chuck beef roast
1 teaspoon salt
½ teaspoon pepper
1 teaspoon thyme
1 bay leaf
1 clove garlic, minced
2 carrots
3 fresh pigs' feet
1 cup red wine
2 envelopes unflavored gelatin
½ cup cold water

Sauté onions in butter in a large kettle or Dutch oven, add beef, and brown. Add seasonings, carrots, pigs' feet, and wine, and cook, tightly covered, on very low heat for 4 to 5 hours. Remove beef to a dish, and remove pigs' feet. Strain broth, removing excess fat. Soften gelatin in cold water, add 1 cup heated broth, and dissolve. Cool. Pour ⅓ of mixture over meat. Decorate top with carrot slices. When set, add 2 more coatings of gelatin, allowing time for setting between each, and refrigerate until serving time. Serves 6 to 8.

SHISH KEBAB

Skewers are required for this recipe (12″ to 15″ length is best)

5 to 6-lb. leg of lamb, cubed
1 15-oz. can small cooked white potatoes, or fresh potatoes, parboiled
2 green peppers, cut in squares
4 tomatoes, quartered
3 small onions, cut into thick slices

MARINADE

¼ **cup salad oil**
⅓ **cup finely chopped onion**
⅓ **cup vinegar**
1 **tablespoon prepared mustard**
1 **teaspoon salt**
⅔ **teaspoon paprika**
2 **cups chili sauce**
2 **tablespoons brown sugar**
1 **clove garlic, minced**

Have butcher cut leg of lamb into 2-inch cubes or do it yourself. Combine all marinade ingredients and place meat in the mixture, stirring to make sure all pieces are covered. Refrigerate for at least 2 hours. String meat onto skewers, alternating with cut-up vegetables, using 3 or 4 pieces of each food to a skewer. Roast 10 to 20 minutes over hot charcoal fire, turning frequently. (If unavailable, skewers may be placed in flat pan, cooked in broiler, and turned frequently to avoid scorching.) Serves 10 to 12.

COLD VITELLO TONNATO*

3½-lb. leg of veal
10 anchovy fillets
½ sour pickle
2 7-oz. cans of tuna fish
1 cup white wine
½ cup olive oil
1 carrot
2 cloves garlic
4 ribs celery
½ teaspoon salt
¼ teaspoon pepper
½ teaspoon thyme
½ teaspoon parsley flakes
4 tablespoons mayonnaise
3 tablespoons capers
4 cups cooked cold rice

Place veal, anchovies, pickle, tuna fish, wine, olive oil, carrot, garlic, celery, and seasonings in covered kettle and simmer for 2 hours. When done, let cool in the pot. Remove veal and purée all ingredients remaining in the pot in electric blender. Add mayonnaise and beat to form a cream. Serve meat sliced thin, topped with the sauce, and garnished with capers, on a bed of cold rice. Serves 8.

STUFFED BREAST OF VEAL*

4 to 6-lb. veal breast
1 clove garlic, minced
1 onion, finely chopped
2 tablespoons vegetable shortening
1½ cups bread cubes
¼ cup chopped parsley
2 lbs. pork sausage meat (buy bulk sausage if possible, or remove casings from sausages)
2 eggs, slightly beaten
¼ cup oatmeal
1 cup tomato sauce

Sauté garlic and onion in shortening briefly, add bread cubes and parsley, and mix. Combine sausage meat, eggs, and oatmeal. Stuff breast of veal with mixture. Close pocket of breast by inserting a piece of aluminum foil and fastening with skewer. Brown the breast in small amount of fat in baking pan. Roast at 325° for 2 hours, basting with tomato sauce and, if necessary, some water. Cool, then refrigerate to serve cold. Serve with anchovy mayonnaise, prepared by combining:

1 cup mayonnaise
1 clove garlic, minced
12 anchovy fillets, chopped
¼ cup capers

Serves 6.

SHRIMP IN MUSTARD SAUCE

3 lbs. shrimp, cooked, shelled, and deveined
1 cup sour cream
1 tablespoon dry mustard
1 teaspoon prepared mustard
2 dashes Tabasco sauce
2 tablespoons capers

Combine all sauce ingredients and add to cleaned, cooked shrimp. Refrigerate 2 hours before serving. Serves 6 to 8.

SHRIMP AND RICE CASSEROLE*

3 cups cooked rice
2 lbs. shrimp, cooked, shelled, and deveined
1 16-oz. can tomatoes
1 green pepper, cut in strips
2 teaspoons salt
¼ teaspoon garlic powder
¼ teaspoon savory

Combine rice, shrimp, tomatoes, and green pepper. Stir in seasonings. Place mixture in 1½-quart casserole and refrigerate several hours. Before serving, bake 30 to 35 minutes at 350°. Serves 4.

JELLIED SALMON WITH CUCUMBER SAUCE

1 fresh salmon (about 3 lbs)
Juice of 1 lemon
½ teaspoon salt
1 medium onion
1 large carrot
1 bunch celery tops
1 parsnip
1 oz. gelatin
2 egg whites
1 cucumber, pared
1 pint sour cream
Green food coloring for cool green tint

Cut salmon into individual portions and sprinkle with lemon juice and salt. Place in casserole. Separately, boil vegetables in a quart of water, until soft, salting to taste. Strain stock and pour over fish. Cook 20 minutes. When done, take out fish and remove skin and bones. Add gelatin to stock, beat, strain through cheesecloth. Add egg whites. Place the fish on a platter and garnish with slices of cooked carrot. When jelly begins to set, pour over fish and refrigerate. Blender-chop cucumber, sour cream, and food coloring, and serve as sauce with fish. Serves 5 to 6.

TOSSED TUNA AND OLIVE SALAD

1 head iceberg lettuce
3 tomatoes, sliced
2 green peppers, cut into strips
3 ribs celery, cut into small pieces
1 small Bermuda or Spanish onion, cut into thin rings
2 7-oz. cans of tuna fish, packed in oil
1 15-oz. can pitted black olives
1 #2 can chickpeas
2 teaspoons oregano
½ teaspoon garlic powder
1 teaspoon salt
¼ teaspoon pepper
½ cup wine vinegar
3 tablespoons salad oil

Wash lettuce and break into bite-sized pieces and add other cut-up vegetables. Break tuna into bite-sized chunks and add, undrained, to salad. Add olives, chickpeas, seasonings, vinegar, and oil, adjusting to taste. Toss lightly. Refrigerate to chill. Serves 6 to 8.

Side Dishes

CARROT RING*

2 cups grated raw carrots
1 cup vegetable shortening
½ cup brown sugar
1 egg
1 tablespoon water
1½ cups flour
½ teaspoon baking powder
½ teaspoon nutmeg
½ teaspoon salt
½ teaspoon cinnamon

Grate carrots, preferably in blender, to make required quantity and set aside. Combine shortening, sugar, egg, and water and blend until creamed. Add this mixture and carrots to dry ingredients and seasonings, and place in refrigerator for at least 5 hours or overnight. Remove from refrigerator ½ hour before baking. Bake in ring mold for 1 hour at 350°. Serves 8.

RICE SALAD

1½ cups rice
1 carrot, chopped
2 ribs celery, chopped
2 scallions, chopped
5 pitted green olives, sliced
5 pitted black olives, sliced
2 small pimientos, cut fine
½ small red onion, chopped
6 tablespoons tarragon vinegar
3 tablespoons salad oil
Salt and pepper

Cook rice according to package instructions. Cool, add remaining ingredients, and toss, adjusting seasonings if desired. Refrigerate to serve 8 to 10.

ASPARAGUS VINAIGRETTE

3 lbs. fresh asparagus stalks, cleaned
½ teaspoon salt
¼ cup tarragon vinegar (lemon juice may be used instead)
¼ teaspoon salt
½ teaspoon prepared mustard
1 clove garlic, crushed in garlic press
1 cup olive oil
1 tablespoon capers

Place asparagus in a saucepan and cover with cold water. Add ½ teaspoon salt, bring to a boil, and cook just 10 minutes to preserve crispness and fresh green color. While asparagus is cooking, mix vinegar with seasonings, stirring rapidly, then add oil and capers, and stir to blend. Pour over hot asparagus and allow to cool, refrigerating for at least 4 hours before serving. Serves 10 to 12.

JELLIED STEWED TOMATOES

2 envelopes unflavored gelatin
½ cup cold water
2 16-oz. cans stewed tomatoes
1 teaspoon oregano

Soften gelatin in ½ cup cold water, using top of double boiler. Place mixture over boiling water and stir until dissolved. Stir gelatin liquid into tomatoes, which have been broken up slightly. Add oregano. Mix thoroughly and pour into 8 6-oz. molds. Refrigerate to set. Serves 8.

LIME AND SOUR CREAM MOLD

1 package lime Jell-o
½ pint sour cream
1 cup grated carrots
1 cup canned crushed pineapple, drained (syrup drained off pineapple may be used in preparation of Jell-o instead of ice water, diluting juice with water to make 1 cup, if necessary)

Prepare Jell-o according to package directions and chill until it begins to thicken. Whip in mixer until fluffy and fold in remaining ingredients. Pour into mold and chill until firm. Serves 8.

CRANBERRY AND NUT MOLD

4 packages raspberry or blackberry Jell-o
4 cups hot water
½ cup red wine
½ cup juice of canned fruit
1 1-lb. can jellied or whole cranberry sauce
1 1-lb. can crushed pineapple or fruit cocktail
½ cup chopped walnuts

Dissolve Jell-o in hot water and add wine and fruit juice. Chill in refrigerator until thickened, then add cranberries, canned fruit, and nuts. Pour into mold and chill. Serves 12.

GRAPEFRUIT MOLD

1 envelope unflavored gelatin
¼ cup cold water
½ cup hot water
½ cup sugar
1 1-lb. can grapefruit sections, drained
3 unpeeled apples, cut into small squares
½ cup walnut pieces

Soften gelatin in cold water, add hot water and sugar, and stir until dissolved. Cool. When partially set, add grapefruit sections, apples, and nuts. Pour into mold and chill in refrigerator until set. Serves 6.

MARINATED CAULIFLOWER

1 medium head cauliflower, cut into florets
2 cups water
1 stem celery, sliced
1 clove garlic, minced
½ teaspoon fennel seed
½ teaspoon thyme
½ bay leaf
8 peppercorns
¾ teaspoon salt
1 cup olive oil
Juice of 3 lemons

Bring all ingredients, except oil and lemon juice, to a boil. Reduce the heat and simmer 5 minutes, stirring occasionally. Turn into a bowl, cool, and add oil and lemon juice. Marinate overnight in refrigerator. Serves 6.

COLE SLAW

3 tablespoons salad oil
2 tablespoons wine vinegar
½ teaspoon garlic powder
½ teaspoon salt
1 teaspoon sugar
1 small head green cabbage, shredded
1 4-oz. jar pimiento, coarsely chopped

Mix together oil, vinegar, and seasonings, and beat until well blended. Add cabbage and drained pimientoes. Mix well and refrigerate covered for several hours or overnight. Drain before serving. Serves 8 to 10.

MARINATED GREEN BEANS

4 cups green beans
½ teaspoon dill seed
1 onion, sliced very thinly
1 large cucumber, thinly sliced and salted
½ clove garlic, minced
1 teaspoon sugar
1 teaspoon paprika
1 teaspoon salt
½ teaspoon pepper
1 teaspoon oregano
2 teaspoons chopped parsley
½ teaspoon prepared mustard
5 tablespoons vinegar
4 tablespoons salad oil

Cook beans in boiling water with dill seed, until just tender. Drain. Some seeds should remain on beans. Add beans to onion and cucumber. Combine remaining ingredients in bowl, mixing well, and pour over vegetables. Allow to marinate in refrigerator overnight. Serves 8.

Desserts

RASPBERRY SOUFFLÉ

½ cup milk
2 envelopes unflavored gelatin
2 eggs
⅓ cup sugar
Dash salt
1 tablespoon lemon juice
1 10-oz. box frozen raspberries, thawed
1 cup heavy cream, whipped

Pour milk in top of double boiler. Add gelatin and place mixture over boiling water to dissolve. Beat eggs with sugar, add salt, lemon juice, and berries. Fold into gelatin mixture. Chill in refrigerator until mixture begins to thicken and then fold in whipped cream. Pour into mold and return to refrigerator to chill several hours, until set. Serves 6.

SHERRY GELATIN

1 package any fruit-flavored gelatin
1¾ cups hot water
3 tablespoons sherry
1 can dark pitted sweet cherries, drained

Dissolve gelatin in hot water, add sherry, and cool. When gelatin begins to set, fold in drained cherries. Chill in refrigerator until firm. Serves 4 to 5.

CHEESE CAKE*

16 to 20 graham crackers, crushed in blender
3 tablespoons melted butter
Dash cinnamon to taste
5 eggs, separated
1 cup sugar
1 lb. cream cheese, room temperature
1 pint sour cream, refrigerator cold
1 teaspoon vanilla
1½ tablespoons lemon juice
1½ teaspoons lemon rind
1½ teaspoons orange rind

Combine crushed graham crackers with melted butter and cinnamon, and line bottom of 10-inch spring form, saving a little to sprinkle over top of cake. Bake at 375° until firm. Cream egg yolks with sugar, add cream cheese, then sour cream, vanilla, lemon juice, and fruit rind. Beat egg whites until stiff but not dry, and gently fold into batter. Pour into crust-lined pan and sprinkle with the rest of the crumbs. Bake at 300° for 1 hour. Turn off the heat, and let cake cool in oven with oven door slightly ajar, for 1 hour. (A folded potholder will hold the door open just enough). Remove cake, and when completely cool, refrigerate for at least 4 hours, taking off sides of cake pan before storing. Serves 10 to 12.

CHEESE CAKE GLAZES

STRAWBERRY

2 to 3 cups fresh strawberries
1 cup water
½ to ¾ cup sugar (according to taste)
1½ tablespoons cornstarch, dissolved in 3 tablespoons cold water

Crush 1 cup strawberries, reserving the rest; add water, and cook 2 minutes. Sieve. Add sugar. Add dissolved cornstarch and stir into hot mixture. Bring to a boil, mixing constantly. Cook until thick and clear. Place whole berries on cake, and top with cooled glaze. Chill in refrigerator.

PINEAPPLE

3 tablespoons sugar
1 tablespoon cornstarch
¼ teaspoon grated lemon rind
1 cup unsweetened pineapple juice

Combine sugar and cornstarch. Stir in lemon rind and pineapple juice. Boil, stirring until clear and thick. Cool to room temperature. Spread on cake, garnishing with pineapple chunks and whipped cream, if desired.

CRANBERRY

1 can whole cranberries
⅓ cup sugar
1 tablespoon cornstarch

Mix sugar with cornstarch, add berries, and cook over low heat until thick and clear. Cool and pour over pie.

PIE CRUST*

1½ cups flour
½ teaspoon baking powder
1 teaspoon salt
½ cup lard or vegetable shortening
¼ cup cold water, approximately

Sift together flour, baking powder, and salt. Using a pastry blender, chop the shortening into the flour until the particles resemble a mixture of coarse meal and peas. Sprinkle water slowly over the top of the flour while tossing the mixture up from the bottom of the bowl with a fork. After about three-fourths of the water has been added, press the dampened part of the dough into a ball and set aside. Add only enough water to dampen the remaining flour. Press all the dough together. Place the ball of dough on a floured board, pat in all directions with a floured rolling pin, and then roll from the center out in all directions, loosening the pastry and re-flouring the board and rolling pin, if necessary. Roll about ⅛ of an inch thick and 2 inches wider than the 9-inch pan. Place pastry in pan, trimming the edge with a sharp knife, a little beyond rim of pan. Flute, if desired. Prick bottom of pastry with a fork to prevent bubbles in the crust. Bake in preheated oven at 450° until delicately brown. Cool, then refrigerate crust.

STRAWBERRY PIE

1 baked 9-inch pie crust (see p. 89)
3 cups fresh strawberries, hulled and washed
¾ cup water
¾ cup sugar
3 tablespoons cornstarch
Red and yellow food coloring (optional)
1 teaspoon lemon juice
½ pint heavy cream, whipped

Simmer 1 cup strawberries with water for 3 minutes. Mix sugar and cornstarch, add to pot, and continue cooking until mixture is clear and thick. Add 1 to 2 drops red and 1 drop yellow food coloring if glaze seems pale. Add lemon juice and cool slightly. Place remaining strawberries in baked pie shell, points up, and pour glaze over them. Chill pie for several hours in refrigerator and serve with whipped cream. Serves 8 to 9.

NOTE: This filling may be used with individual tarts as well as for a whole pie. To make 15 2-inch tarts, prepare double the pie crust recipe (p. 89).

PEACH PIE

1 baked 9-inch pie crust (see p. 89)
3 cups fresh peaches (about 12 peaches)
1 tablespoon lemon juice
¾ cup water
¾ cup sugar
3 tablespoons cornstarch
1 teaspoon lemon juice

Immerse peaches in boiling water for a few minutes until skins slip off easily. Slice peaches in crescents and sprinkle with lemon juice. Simmer 1 cup peaches (about 4 peaches) with ¾ cup water for 3 minutes. Mix sugar and cornstarch, add to pot, and continue cooking until mixture is clear and thick. Add lemon juice and cool slightly. Place remaining peaches in baked pie shell and pour glaze over them. Chill pie for several hours in refrigerator. Serves 8 to 9.

BLACK CHERRY PIE

1 baked 9-inch pie crust (see p. 89)
2 #2½ cans pitted red Bing cherries
Juice of ½ lemon
Dash salt and sugar
1 teaspoon almond flavoring
1 tablespoon cornstarch per each cup of juice
½ pint heavy sweet cream
1 tablespoon gelatin, softened in ⅓ cup of water

Drain juice from canned cherries, and add to it the lemon, dash of salt, dash of sugar, almond flavoring, and 1 tablespoon of cornstarch per each cup of juice. Boil until spoon is coated and glaze is clear. Let cool.

Whip heavy cream, folding in gelatin softened in water, and, if desired, a bit of sugar to taste. Pour this whipped cream mixture into baked pie shell. Place cherries over it. Top with cooled juice glaze and refrigerate to set. Do not keep more than a day. Serves 8 to 10.

CRANBERRY-PUMPKIN CHIFFON PIE*

1 baked 9-inch pie crust (see p. 89)
1 tablespoon unflavored gelatin
4 tablespoons cold water
1 cup fresh cranberries
½ cup chopped raisins
6 tablespoons sugar
1 tablespoon grated orange rind
2 eggs, separated
¾ cup sugar
¼ teaspoon salt
½ teaspoon nutmeg
½ teaspoon cinnamon
1 cup canned pumpkin
⅓ cup milk

Soften half of the gelatin in 2 tablespoons of cold water and set over hot water to dissolve. Coarsely chop cranberries and raisins in blender. Add sugar, grated orange rind, and gelatin. Let stand to thicken. Spread in bottom of pie shell and chill in refrigerator until firm.

In top of double boiler, beat egg yolks with ½ cup of sugar, salt, nutmeg, and cinnamon. Mash pumpkin and stir into egg mixture, adding the milk. Cook over hot water, stirring constantly, until thick. Remove from heat. Soften remaining gelatin in remaining 2 tablespoons of cold water and add to pumpkin mixture. Chill over ice water until thick, stirring frequently. Beat egg whites until in soft peaks, add remaining ¼ cup sugar, and beat until stiff but not dry. Fold into chilled pumpkin mixture. Pour over cranberries in pie shell. Chill until firm. If desired, serve with whipped cream. Serves 8.

BRANDY PIE

1 package unflavored gelatin
¼ cup brandy
2 eggs, separated
1¼ cups milk
¾ cup sugar
½ teaspoon salt
2 teaspoons instant coffee
1 teaspoon vanilla
¼ teaspoon cream of tartar
½ pint heavy cream, whipped
1 cup walnuts, chopped fine
1 dozen ladyfingers, split

Soak gelatin in brandy. In top of double boiler, combine egg yolks, milk, ½ cup of sugar, salt, and instant coffee. Stir over boiling water until mixture coats spoon, then add brandy-gelatin mixture, and stir until dissolved. Add vanilla. Chill until slightly thickened. Beat egg whites with cream of tartar until light. Add ¼ cup of sugar and whipped cream to gelatin mixture until well blended. Add ¾ cup chopped walnuts and fold in. Butter a 10-inch glass pie plate and line sides and bottom with ladyfingers. Pour pie filling over ladyfingers. Garnish with remaining chopped nuts. Chill well before cutting. Serves 10.

BLUEBERRY TART

1 baked 9-inch pie crust (see p. 89), refrigerated to chill
1 quart fresh blueberries
1 12-oz. jar currant jelly
2 teaspoons lemon juice
2 tablespoons butter
½ pint heavy sweet cream, whipped

Wash the berries, picking them over and discarding damaged ones. Dry with a terry towel, rubbing just enough to slightly bruise the fruit. Refrigerate to chill well. Melt the currant jelly in the top of a double boiler. Add lemon juice and stir. Rub chilled pie shell with butter. Pour in blueberries and distribute evenly. Pour hot, melted currant jelly over the fruit and refrigerate until chilled and set. Before serving, decorate with whipped cream. Serves 6 to 8.

BLUEBERRY DESSERT

1 cup plus 2 tablespoons sifted flour
Pinch of salt
1 cup plus 2 tablespoons sugar
½ cup butter
1 tablespoon white vinegar
Dash cinnamon
3 cups fresh blueberries
Confectioners' sugar for sprinkling

Combine 1 cup flour, salt, and 2 tablespoons sugar. Work in butter with pastry blender. Stir in vinegar. Spread dough in 9-inch round spring-form pan that is 1½ inches deep. Make bottom crust ¼ inch thick, spreading the sides more thinly to the height of 1 inch. Combine 1 cup sugar, 2 tablespoons flour, and the cinnamon. Add 2 cups blueberries. Pour into crust. Bake at 400° for 1 hour. Remove from oven and put 1 cup uncooked berries on top. Cool, remove rim of pan. Sprinkle with confectioners' sugar and decorate with whipped cream, if desired. Chill to serve. Serves 6 to 8.

PEACH KUCHEN*

2 cups flour
¼ teaspoon baking powder
½ teaspoon salt
¼ lb. plus 2 tablespoons butter
2 large cans peach halves
½ cup cinnamon and sugar mixture
1½ cups sour cream
2 egg yolks

Combine first 3 ingredients. Cut in butter with knife or pastry blender. Pat dough into bottom and sides of square greased pan 8 x 8 x 2 inches, about ½ inch thick. Drain canned peaches and place fruit cut-side-down on pastry, overlapping if necessary. Sprinkle with cinnamon and suger mixture. Bake at 350° for 20 minutes. Remove from oven and top cake with 1½ cups sour cream which has been beaten with 2 egg yolks. Return to oven and bake 40 minutes more. Chill in refrigerator. Serves 6 to 8.

APRICOT REFRIGERATOR CAKE*

1 lb. dried apricots
2 cups water
1 cup butter
2 cups confectioners' sugar, sifted
4 eggs, separated
Grated rind and juice of 1 lemon
⅓ cup granulated sugar
36 ladyfingers
¾ cup heavy cream, whipped
Toasted sliced almonds

Simmer apricots in water until tender and all water has been absorbed. Mash to make pulp (blender is excellent for this), and cool. Cream butter, add confectioners' sugar, and beat until light. Add egg yolks one at a time, and beat well. Beat in apricot pulp, lemon rind, and juice. Beat egg whites until stiff, add sugar, and continue beating until sugar is dissolved. Fold into apricot mixture. Line deep 9-inch spring-form pan with ladyfingers, split. Layer alternately one-third of the mixture and one-third of the lady-fingers. Chill at least overnight. Remove sides of pan and garnish with whipped cream and almonds. Stores well in refrigerator for several days. Serves 10 to 12.

REFRIGERATOR COOKIES*

½ lb. sweet butter
1 8-oz. package cream cheese
½ lb. all-purpose flour
Strawberry jam
2 egg whites
½ cup crushed walnuts, mixed with ¼ cup sugar

Allow butter and cheese to soften a little at room temperature. Mix them together well, add flour, roll into ball, and chill at least overnight. Roll out one-half of the dough on well-floured board, and cut out circles with a glass. Spread circles with jam. Place on cookie sheet and set aside. Roll remaining one-half of dough, cut circles as above, then cut out centers of each with thimble or similar small object. Dip tops of these in egg white, then the sugar and nut mixture, and place on top of jam circles. Bake 10 to 12 minutes at 300°, or until golden.

NOTE: This dough may be rolled out flat, spread with jam, nuts, raisins, or any filling of your choice, and rolled jelly-roll fashion to bake. When slightly cooled, roll is sliced for pinwheel cookies.

PAVÉ AU CHOCOLAT

1 6-oz. package semisweet chocolate bits
½ cup very hot coffee
4 eggs, separated
2 tablespoons rum or cognac
1 envelope unflavored gelatin, softened in 2 tablespoons of water
½ cup cold water
2 packages ladyfingers (2 dozen)
½ pint heavy cream, whipped

Combine chocolate with hot coffee (blender is excellent for this) until chocolate is dissolved. Add beaten yolks, rum, and gelatin and mix well. (If using blender, just add these ingredients to chocolate mixture and blend.) Meanwhile, beat egg whites until stiff. Fold chocolate mixture into egg whites, distributing well. Combine 2 tablespoons rum with cold water. Halve ladyfingers, and one at a time, dip them in this liquid. Place in wheel-spoke fashion on bottom of layer or tube pan which has been lined with wax paper. (You will have to do this quickly as ladyfingers will tend to disintegrate.) Spread ladyfinger layer with one-half of filling. Add another layer of ladyfingers, proceding as above, and then remainder of filling. Chill very thoroughly. To serve, run knife around edge of pan, and turn out. Wax paper on bottom of pan will make pavé slide out easily. Decorate with whipped cream. Serves 8.

SOUR CREAM CHOCOLATE CAKE*

2 squares unsweetened chocolate
½ cup water
2 cups cake flour, sifted
1 teaspoon baking soda
Pinch salt
⅓ cup butter
1½ cups sugar
3 eggs
1 teaspoon vanilla
1 cup sour cream

Melt chocolate with water in double boiler until it forms smooth paste. Cool. Sift flour, soda, and salt together and set aside. Cream butter, add sugar gradually, and add eggs. Mix well. Blend in chocolate and vanilla. Add sifted flour mix and sour cream alternately. Grease and flour 2 9-inch pans. Bake at 325° for 35 to 40 minutes.

FROSTING

1½ cups heavy cream
¼ cup sugar
2 tablespoons cocoa
½ teaspoon vanilla

Mix, do not whip, all ingredients. Chill 2 hours, then whip.

CHOCOLATE ANGEL PIE

2 egg whites
Dash salt
⅛ teaspoon cream of tartar
½ cup granulated sugar
½ cup chopped walnuts
½ teaspoon vanilla
1 package semisweet chocolate bits
3 tablespoons water
1 teaspoon vanilla
½ cup heavy cream, whipped

Beat egg whites with rotary beater until foamy. Add salt and
cream of tartar. Continue beating until mixture will stand in soft
peaks. Add sugar gradually and continue beating until very stiff.
Fold in nuts; add ½ teaspoon vanilla. Turn into lightly greased
8-inch pie pan. Build up sides. Bake at 300° for 50 or 55 minutes.
Cool. Place chocolate and water in saucepan over low heat and
stir until it becomes melted. Cool, add 1 teaspoon vanilla, and
fold in whipped cream. Put in meringue shell. Chill 2 hours
before using. Additional whipped cream may be served on top of
pie, if desired. Serves 6.

MANDARIN ORANGE AMBROSIA PIE

AMBROSIA PIE CRUST

2 tablespoons softened butter
2 cups flaked coconut

MANDARIN ORANGE FILLING

1 11-oz. can mandarin orange segments
1 1-lb. 4-oz. can pineapple slices, cut into pieces
1 cup miniature marshmallows
½ cup shredded coconut
½ pint sour cream

Spread softened butter over bottom and sides of an 8-inch pie plate. Pat coconut flakes evenly against butter-lined pie plate. Bake in 300° oven 15 to 20 minutes until coconut is toasted. Remove from oven and let cool. Chill in refrigerator until cold. Meanwhile, drain juice from orange segments and pineapple and combine fruit with remaining ingredients. Chill. Spoon into cold pie shell and serve immediately. Serves 8.

REFRIGERATOR ROLL-UPS*

½ lb. butter
½ cup sugar
2 egg yolks
½ cup sour cream
2 teaspoons baking powder
2½ cups flour
**Chopped nuts mixed with cinnamon and sugar, jam, or coconut as
  desired for filling**

Mix together butter, sugar, and egg yolks. Add sour cream, baking powder, and flour. Work all together with hands. Dough will be sticky. Chill overnight. Roll out half the dough, ¼ inch thick. Cut into 2-inch squares. Place 1 tablespoon of chopped nuts, cinnamon, and sugar mixture in the center of each square. Roll diagonally from one point to another. Roll out remaining dough and fill with jam and/or coconut. Roll up in one long strip. Bake roll-ups at 350° until brown. Cut long roll into pieces while warm. Yields about 60 roll-ups.

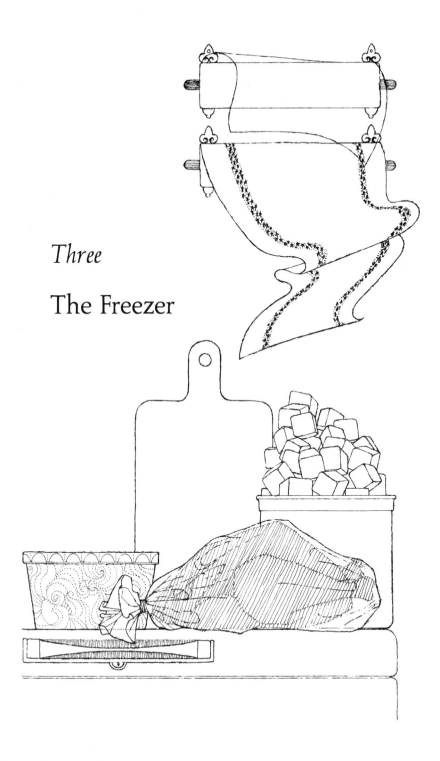

Three

The Freezer

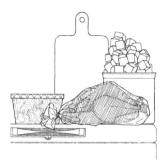

The Freezer

When I first began using the freezer, I looked upon it primarily as a storage box for meats and commercially packaged frozen foods. It was wonderful to cut down on shopping and menu-planning time. I still liked it even after the chicken which I had so hurriedly pushed into the freezer one day fell on my toe and broke it when next I opened the door. I soon realized that intelligent distribution of foods is an essential aspect of freezer enjoyment. More so, however, I learned that for greatest economy and time-saving, I should plan ahead and store cooked foods for later use.

Using the freezer in this way, I discovered what a joy it could really be. Although it's nice when you're late for dinner to know that there is a steak in the freezer that can be popped into the broiler in a few seconds, it is the eggplant caviar, the orzo in mushroom sauce, and the pecan strips you made and froze last week that make your hurried meal an occasion instead of an afterthought. While you're heating your sumptuous meal and preparing the salad that will complete it, chill a bottle of wine and drink a toast to your freezer. It helps you to be a gracious impromptu hostess and justifiably earns you the reputation of excellent cook and efficient organizer.

The freezer allows you maximum flexibility: you can cook when the mood strikes you; it frees you from routine; and it offers you the opportunity to serve more varied and interesting meals. It is a great help when you have to cope with unforeseen difficulties —adverse weather, illness, unexpected company. Time limitations no longer matter: if you're home anyway and are puttering in the kitchen, it means nothing if you take two hours to reheat a frozen casserole; but if you know that you'll be out all day and coming home to guests, take the frozen casserole out to defrost at room temperature before you leave in the morning, and reheat the contents in the half-hour it takes you to coordinate the rest of the meal in the evening. In short, the freezer can make you a creative and relaxed cook and hostess, whether your meal is a spur-of-the-moment occasion or a formally planned affair.

Throughout the book, all recipes which lend themselves to freezing have been marked with asterisks. In this chapter, the emphasis is on the intentional cook-aheads—all to be frozen, requiring only that you heat-and-serve or defrost and serve.

A word of caution: in reheating frozen dishes, always start with a cold oven—this prevents warped or cracked cooking utensils and scorched foods!

NOTE: As freezer temperatures are likely to vary somewhat, so does the time necessary for reheating, especially casserole dishes. Thus, I have specified only the minimum time required for reheating. The crucial test is that edges are bubbly and center of prepared dish is as soft and hot as its outer rim.

Appetizers

CHEESE BALL IN NUTS*

1 3-oz. package cream cheese, softened
6 oz. blue cheese
3 oz. processed American cheese
¼ cup light cream
1 teaspoon onion juice or chopped onion
2 teaspoons Worcestershire sauce
½ cup walnuts, chopped

Mix all ingredients except nuts until well blended. Wrap in aluminum foil, molding into a round ball. Chill until firm enough to handle, then roll in nuts. Rewrap and freeze until needed. Makes about one 6-inch ball. Serve at room temperature. Allow at least 3 hours for defrosting.

QUICK PATÉ*

1 lb. liverwurst (the soft, spreadable type)
½ cup very soft butter
½ cup brandy

Blend all ingredients and mellow in refrigerator at least overnight, or freeze and then defrost in refrigerator a day before serving to allow for blending of flavors. Serves 8 to 10.

EGGPLANT CAVIAR*

1 large eggplant
1 green pepper
½ small onion, chopped fine
1 teaspoon salt
½ teaspoon garlic powder
¼ teaspoon pepper
3 tablespoons lemon juice
¼ cup olive oil

Bake unpeeled eggplant and green pepper in 300° oven for 40 minutes until soft and collapsed. Remove skin from eggplant and seeds from green pepper. Chop fine, combine with remaining ingredients, and adjust seasonings to taste. Drain and freeze in plastic container. To serve, remove from freezer 4 hours before serving. Serve cold. Serves 10.

NOTE: If smoky flavor is desired, scorch eggplant and green pepper directly over range burner (gas or electric are fine) and turn until skin is charred on all sides. Turn into pan and bake as above, following remaining directions.

EGGPLANT SAUTÉ*

1 large eggplant, unpeeled and cut in cubes
1 green pepper, seeded
1 large onion, finely chopped
¼ cup olive oil or salad oil
1 6-oz. can tomato paste
2 tablespoons chili sauce
2 tablespoons ketchup
2 tablespoons lemon juice
¼ cup stuffed olives
4 to 5 small green Italian hot peppers (or less according to taste)
½ teaspoon oregano
⅛ teaspoon ground pepper

Sauté eggplant, sweet pepper, and onion in salad oil until glossy. Add remaining ingredients and simmer, covered, until eggplant is tender, about 30 minutes. Cool. Freeze in plastic container. Serve cold. Makes enough to serve 12 to 14.

ROQUEFORT BALLS*

¼ lb. Roquefort cheese, at room temperature
1 teaspoon soft butter
1 teaspoon Worcestershire sauce
1 teaspoon brandy
1 tablespoon chopped parsley

Mix together all ingredients in blender. Roll into balls, garnish or roll in chopped parsley or paprika, and freeze until needed. Serve at room temperature. Serves 10 to 12.

FILLED CANAPÉS*

PASTRY

NOTE: This pastry is made in 2 parts, which are then joined together by rolling, folding and rolling again, repeating this operation several times.

Part I
1 lb. butter
2 cups flour

Cut butter into flour with a pastry blender. Knead and refrigerate to chill thoroughly.

Part II
2 cups flour
2 egg yolks
½ pint sour cream
1½ teaspoons white vinegar

Combine ingredients of Part II and roll out on floured board. Place butter-and-flour pastry on top, fold bottom dough over it on all sides, and flatten by rolling. Fold all 4 sides towards middle and roll flat at least 6 to 7 more times. Separate into several sections and refrigerate or freeze until ready to use. To bake, roll each section about ¼ inch thick, spread with filling, roll up jelly-roll fashion, and bake at 350° for 45 minutes. Slice for pinwheel canapés when slightly cool. For main course, make thicker roll and bake in one piece. Cut servings to desired length. Makes 50 to 60 hot canapés, or will serve 10 as a main course.

CABBAGE FILLING*

1 medium-sized head of cabbage
¼ lb. butter
¼ cup milk or half-and-half (half milk and half cream)
Salt and pepper to taste
3 hard-boiled eggs, chopped fine
2 tablespoons chopped fresh dill

Shred cabbage. Place in large kettle, pour boiling water over it, and cook for 2 minutes. Drain; then squeeze dry with hands. Return to pot, add butter, milk or cream, and salt and pepper, and steam, covered, until soft. Add chopped hard-boiled eggs and dill and mix well.

MEAT FILLING*

½ lb. chopped meat
½ small onion
2 tablespoons butter
⅛ teaspoon garlic
¼ teaspoon salt
Dash pepper
1 tablespoon chopped fresh dill

Sauté meat and onions in butter. Run through meat grinder twice. Add seasonings. Spread over rolled-out dough, then roll up and slice into pinwheels, or fill individual round disks, folding over into half-moons and sealing edges by pressing together with fork tines, or fill according to the instructions on page 110.

LIVER AND LUNG FILLING*

1 small onion, chopped
1 lb. beef lung, boiled and chopped (sometimes called "lights"—a
  special request to butcher may be necessary)
5 chicken livers, finely cut
2 tablespoons shortening
1 egg, beaten
1 teaspoon salt
¼ teaspoon pepper

Sauté onion, lung, and chicken livers in shortening until brown.
Mix with egg and seasonings. Use to fill pastry as with Meat Filling.

CRAB MEAT CREAM PUFFS*

CREAM PUFFS

1 cup water
½ cup vegetable shortening
1 cup flour
3 eggs

Boil water with shortening in saucepan; then throw in flour all at
once, and stir vigorously, until the mass comes away from the pot.
Cool. Stir in the eggs, one at a time. With a spoon drop dough on
greased cookie sheet, using ½ teaspoon if miniature canapés are
desired. If dessert-sized cream puffs are desired, use a tablespoon.
Bake at 450° for 20 minutes, then at 350° for another 15 minutes,
or until golden brown. Cool and split puffs with sharp knife to fill.
Makes about 40 to 50 miniatures, or 12 large puffs.

CRAB MEAT FILLING*

2 6½-oz. cans crab meat
3 tablespoons mayonnaise
2 tablespoons chopped dill pickle
¼ teaspoon monosodium glutamate

Rinse crab meat under cold water. Mix all ingredients together. Fill cream puffs. Place on cookie sheet and freeze until firm; then wrap to store. Heat in moderate oven for 10 to 15 minutes to serve hot.

BEEF PASTRY ROLL-UPS*

For pastry, see "Hot Pastry Canapés," page 12.

1 lb. ground chuck
½ small onion, chopped
2 tablespoons butter
1 tablespoon chopped parsley
1 teaspoon salt
⅛ teaspoon pepper
½ cup beef stock
2 tablespoons flour

Brown meat and onion in butter, add seasonings, and then stir in stock and flour, cooking until thickened. Cool. Spread on dough rolled about ¼ inch thick. Roll up dough and slice into ¾-inch pieces, to form pinwheels. Bake on ungreased cookie sheet at 350° for about 20 minutes. Cool and wrap to freeze. Makes 30 to 40.

NOTE: Pastry dough and filling may be frozen separately, or assembled, cut ¼ inch thick, and placed on cookie sheet in freezer, unbaked. When firm, remove from sheet, stack, wrap, and keep frozen until ready to use. To serve, place frozen canapés on cookie sheet and bake at 350° about 30 to 40 minutes, or until golden brown. Serve hot.

PHYLLO TRIANGLES*

1 lb. ricotta cheese
½ lb. feta cheese
2 eggs
1 lb. phyllo dough (strudel leaves) (if purchased frozen, defrost to use)
¾ lb. butter

Mix together cheese and eggs. Unfold strudel leaves and cut into 2-inch strips, cutting the full length of the sheets of pastry. Melt butter, and with a pastry brush brush surface of each 2-inch strip with melted butter. Drop ½ teaspoon of cheese filling at bottom end of strip. Lifting left corner of single leaf, fold diagonally just enough to cover cheese filling. Lift opposite corner (right) and fold diagonally towards the left. Continue to form in this fashion (in the manner of folding the American flag) to the end of the strip. Repeat for each strip until cheese and strudel leaves are used up. Spread any pastry remains with blue cheese mixed with butter and minced onion flakes and roll into 2-inch canapés. Bake at 350° for 20 minutes. Serves 14 to 16.

NOTE: To freeze, spread unbaked canapés on cookie sheet and place in freezer until firm. Store wrapped or in covered container until needed. Do not bake before freezing. To serve, place frozen canapés on cookie sheet, defrost slightly, and bake at 350° for 30 to 40 minutes or until canapés are golden and puffed up.

BARBECUED SPARERIBS*

3 lbs. spareribs
3 cups water
½ cup white vinegar
¾ cup minced onion
1 clove garlic, minced
1½ tablespoons Worcestershire sauce
¾ cup brown sugar
5 tablespoons ketchup
1 tablespoon salt
5 tablespoons salad oil
¼ teaspoon pepper
1 bay leaf

Broil spareribs until golden brown on both sides. Meanwhile, combine remaining ingredients and boil for 10 minutes in uncovered saucepan. Place spareribs in a 10 x 15 x 2-inch baking pan and pour some of the sauce over them. Bake in hot oven at 450° for 1 hour, basting every 10 minutes with remaining sauce, which should be kept boiling hot. Serve hot. Serves 5 to 6.

NOTE: To freeze, broiled ribs and boiled sauce may be frozen separately. When ready to serve, defrost for 3 hours, combine in baking pan and proceed as above, heating remaining sauce for basting separately.

If you prefer, you may combine ribs and sauce before freezing. When ready to serve, place frozen in baking pan in 350° oven for 1 hour. Increase temperature to 400° and bake an additional ½ hour, basting frequently.

Soups

BORSCHT*

2 lbs. soup meat (beef brisket, shin, or other soup meat)
2 tablespoons shortening
2 large onions
2 quarts water
1 bunch soup greens (celery, parsley, leek, etc.)
2 teaspoons salt
¼ teaspoon pepper
1 1-lb. 4-oz. can tomatoes
1 1-lb. 4-oz. can shoestring sliced beets
2 tablespoons white vinegar
1 pint sour cream

Brown meat in shortening in large soup kettle. Add onion and sauté. Add 2 quarts of water, cleaned soup greens tied in a bunch for easy removal, and salt and pepper. Simmer until meat is tender. Add undrained tomatoes and beets to which 2 tablespoons white vinegar have been added (to preserve color) and simmer again until hot. Cool before freezing. Do not fill storage containers to the top—frozen liquid will expand and may force off lid if too full. When ready to serve, stand container in hot water until frozen block is ready to slip out. Transfer to soup kettle and heat until near boiling. Cut meat into portions and return to soup. Serve with sour cream. Serves 8 to 10.

OLD-FASHIONED VEGETABLE SOUP*

3 lbs. soup meat (brisket, shin, or other soup meat)
2 marrow bones
3 quarts of water
2 teaspoons salt
¼ teaspoon pepper
1 onion, diced
4 carrots, diced
4 potatoes, diced
1 large can whole tomatoes
1 small head of cabbage, shredded
1 cup corn kernels

Sear meat in heavy kettle, add soup bones, water, and salt and pepper. Simmer until meat is tender. Add vegetables and simmer another ½ hour. Cool and drain off fat before filling containers for freezing. Serves 10 to 12.

CABBAGE SOUP*

1 small head cabbage
1 tablespoon salt
1 onion, minced
2 tablespoons oil
2 quarts beef stock
Juice of 2 lemons
¼ cup brown sugar
2 cups tomato juice
1 teaspoon salt

Shred cabbage, sprinkle with salt, and let stand at least 1 hour. In kettle, sauté onion in oil. Pour boiling water over cabbage, drain, then place in kettle with beef stock, lemon juice, sugar, tomato juice, and salt. Cover and simmer until cabbage is tender (about

45 minutes). Serves 8. To freeze, do not fill storage container too full. When ready to serve, loosen frozen block by standing in hot water. Transfer to soup kettle, and reheat.

LIVER DUMPLING SOUP*

1 lb. fresh beef liver, ground (use blender)
2 medium onions, sliced
2 tablespoons butter
2 slices stale bread
2 tablespoons chopped parsley
1 teaspoon salt
⅛ teaspoon pepper
¼ teaspoon nutmeg
1½ quarts beef or chicken broth

Sauté onions in butter. Soak bread in a solution of half water and half milk, then squeeze dry. Combine ground liver, sautéed onions, soaked bread, and seasonings. Drop by rounded spoonfuls into boiling broth and simmer 5 to 10 minutes. Serves 4 to 6. To freeze, do not fill storage container too full. When ready to serve, loosen frozen block by standing in hot water. Transfer to soup kettle, and reheat.

ONION SOUP*

4 large onions, sliced thinly and separated into rings
3 tablespoons butter
1½ quarts beef stock
⅛ clove garlic
1 teaspoon salt
⅛ teaspoon pepper
6 slices French bread, toasted
3 tablespoons grated Parmesan cheese

Brown onion rings in butter. Add broth and seasonings. Simmer until onions are tender. Freeze in large container when cool. To serve, heat, then pour soup into individual earthenware crocks, arrange a slice of French bread on each, sprinkle cheese on toast, and place under broiler until cheese melts and browns. Serves 6.

Main Dishes

CHICKEN SAUTÉ WITH MUSHROOM SAUCE*

1 roasting chicken (3½ lbs.) cut up
3 tablespoons salad oil
1 clove garlic, minced
½ lb. fresh mushrooms, thinly sliced
3 tablespoons butter
5 scallions, thinly sliced
¼ cup chopped fresh chives
1 cup dry white wine
1 teaspoon salt
¼ teaspoon pepper
3 slices white bread

Heat salad oil, add garlic, and brown. Add chicken, brown on all sides, then cover and cook slowly until tender (about 1 hour). In another pan, sauté mushrooms in butter for 5 minutes, add scallions, chives, wine, and seasonings, and simmer 10 minutes. Pour over chicken to serve, or freeze separately from chicken. Cut bread into small cubes and fry in butter until golden to make croutons. Freeze separately from chicken. To serve, heat chicken in oven; heat sauce in saucepan. Heat croutons in oven. Arrange chicken on platter; pour sauce over it; garnish with croutons. Serves 4 to 6.

CHICKEN BREASTS WITH POTATO STUFFING*

4 chicken breasts, boned and split
1 large onion, chopped
3 ribs celery, chopped
¼ lb. butter
4 cups mashed potatoes
2 eggs, slightly beaten
1 cup herb-seasoned bread stuffing
¼ cup chopped parsley
1 teaspoon salt
¼ teaspoon pepper
¼ cup melted butter
½ teaspoon salt
Dash pepper
¼ teaspoon paprika

Sauté onion and celery in butter just until tender; add to mashed potatoes. Stir in eggs, stuffing, parsley, salt, and pepper. Turn into greased shallow baking dish. Arrange chicken breasts on top of mixture, brush with melted butter and season. Bake in 350° oven 40 to 45 minutes, or until chicken is tender and golden. Serves 6 to 8.

NOTE: Potatoes should be prepared just before serving. Chicken breasts may be pre-baked and frozen. When ready to serve, defrost chicken (about 3 hours), place over potatoes and bake at 350° for 20 minutes.

ARROZ CON POLLO*

2 frying chickens, about 2½ lbs. each, cut as for frying
½ cup olive oil
1 teaspoon salt
¼ teaspoon pepper
¼ teaspoon saffron, combined with ½ cup hot water (let stand 1
    hour, then simmer about 10 minutes, strain, and use liquid)
1 large onion, cut up
1 clove garlic, minced
½ lb. fresh mushrooms, sliced
1 green pepper, cut in strips
1 2-oz. jar sliced pimientos
1½ cups uncooked rice

STOCK

6 to 7 cups water
2 ribs celery
1 large onion
1 teaspoon salt
¼ teaspoon pepper
Gizzards, necks, bony parts of chickens, and tips of wings

Simmer stock ingredients for 1½ hours. Strain.

In large skillet, sauté chicken in half the oil until golden. Add half
the stock, salt, pepper, and the strained saffron liquid. Cover, and
simmer about 25 minutes. In heavy casserole dish, sauté onion,
garlic, mushrooms, green pepper, and pimiento in remaining
oil. Add rice and liquid and sauté until rice is evenly golden. Add
chicken on top of rice mixture, cover, and cook about 30 minutes,
or until rice and chicken are tender. To serve, place rice in center
of serving platter, and arrange chicken around it. Serves 6 to 8.

NOTE: This may be frozen either by keeping chicken and rice
separated or by arranging them together in the same large casserole

in which the meal will be heated in the oven and served. If defrosted, heat at 350° for 30 minutes. However, you may prefer to put frozen casserole in 325° oven and bake for 1¼ hours.

CHICKEN ROYAL*

3 broiling chickens, split in half
½ cup heavy cream
1½ teaspoons salt
¼ teaspoon pepper
¾ cup white wine
½ lb. fresh mushrooms, chopped fine
2 tablespoons butter
⅓ cup cream
½ cup blanched almonds, blender-ground very fine to a meal
1 tablespoon chopped parsley

If broilers are whole, split in half. Brush with some of the heavy cream, covering very well. Season birds. Cover bottom of large baking pan with wine. Arrange chicken in it without overlapping. Bake at 325° for 60 minutes, basting several times, leaving uncovered for even browning. Sauté chopped mushrooms in butter. Add remaining cream. Add ground almonds and stir until mixture thickens and becomes fluffy. Drop this puffed-up mixture by spoonfuls into spaces between chickens. Sprinkle with parsley. Turn oven down to 250° and keep warm until ready to serve. Serves 6.

NOTE: To freeze, store chicken after it has been baked in wine, but omit preparation of almond puffs until serving time. To serve, heat frozen chicken until sizzling and crisp, then proceed as above.

CHICKEN LOAF*

5 chicken breasts, with skin and bone removed
1 cup corn flakes
1 cup cold milk
2 eggs
2 carrots, ground
1 teaspoon salt
¼ teaspoon pepper
1 teaspoon parsley flakes
1 teaspoon dill weed

In meat-grinding attachment of electric mixer, grind chicken meat. Soak corn flakes in milk and add to meat. Beat eggs slightly and mix in. Add remaining ingredients and mix well. Pack mixture into 9 x 5 x 3-inch loaf pan and cover with aluminum foil. Bake at 350° for 1¼ hours. Remove aluminum foil after first ½ hour, baste, and continue baking uncovered. Serves 6 to 8.

NOTE: Freeze wrapped in aluminum foil. To serve, leave in foil and heat frozen loaf at 325° for 50 minutes.

TURKEY SAUTERNE*

4 lbs. turkey pieces or rolled turkey roast
½ cup sifted flour
1½ teaspoons salt
¼ teaspoon paprika
½ cup butter
1 cup sauterne
1½ cups chicken broth
1 clove garlic, minced
1 teaspoon dry basil
½ lb. fresh mushrooms, sliced

Cut turkey into serving pieces, or slice roast into ¼-inch slices. Combine flour, salt, and paprika, and coat turkey with mixture. Melt ½ the butter in heavy skillet, and brown meat. Place in shallow casserole. Combine wine, broth, garlic, and basil. Pour over turkey and bake at 350° for 45 minutes. Sauté mushrooms in remaining ½ of butter, add to casserole, and continue baking for another 45 minutes. Serves 6.

NOTE: Freeze in casserole. To serve, reheat frozen casserole in 350° oven and bake 65 minutes.

TEA-ORANGE DUCKLING*

1 duckling
1 cup strong tea
¼ cup honey
2 tablespoons soy sauce
2 oranges

Roast duckling at 350° for 1½ hours. Drain off fat. Increase oven temperature to 425°. Combine tea with honey, soy sauce, and oranges, which have been peeled and sectioned. Do not discard orange peel. Pour tea mixture over duckling, and roast for 1 hour more, basting periodically with tea-honey mixture. Dismember duck into serving pieces and place on serving platter. Serve with orange sauce. Serves 4.

NOTE: Freeze in casserole. To serve, reheat frozen casserole in container and frozen until ready to use, but sauce should be prepared just before serving, as freezing will make it turn cloudy. Freezing will not affect taste of sauce. When ready to serve, duck should be defrosted and reheated at 350° for 30 minutes.

ORANGE SAUCE

2 tablespoons orange peel, cut into thin slivers
2 tablespoons sugar
¼ cup red wine vinegar
¾ cup water
1 chicken bouillon cube
½ cup orange juice
2 cloves
1 tablespoon tomato ketchup
1 tablespoon cornstarch
¼ cup medium sherry

In saucepan, cover slivered orange peel with cold water and boil 10 minutes. Drain off water and reserve peel. Combine sugar and vinegar in small saucepan and boil 3 minutes until sugar caramelizes and turns brown. Add water, bouillon cube, orange juice, cloves, and ketchup and simmer about 5 minutes. Blend cornstarch with sherry and stir into sauce. Cook and stir until clear and thickened. Remove cloves from sauce and add slivered orange peel. Serve sauce separately to be spooned over servings of duck.

JAMBALAYA*

¼ lb. slice of ham
¼ lb. slab cured bacon
2 tablespoons salad oil
3 medium onions, chopped
1½ lbs. mushrooms, sliced
1 clove garlic, minced
2 cups uncooked rice
2 cups beef stock
½ cup water
4 fresh tomatoes, peeled and chopped
1 bay leaf
¼ teaspoon saffron, soaked in ¼ cup hot water
½ cup white wine
½ cup red wine
1 lb. raw shrimp, shelled and deveined

Dice ham and bacon into cubes. Heat oil, and sauté ham and bacon in it until brown. Add onions, mushrooms, and garlic, and cook in fat until shiny and limp. Add rice and brown. Add beef stock, water, tomatoes, bay leaf, and saffron. Cook until some of the liquid is absorbed, then add wine and place shrimp on top. Do not stir. Cover and cook until rice is tender, about 30 minutes. Freeze in heat-and-serve covered casserole, and heat frozen casserole thoroughly before serving, at 350° for 45 to 50 minutes. Serves 6.

VEAL PAPRIKASH*

4 to 5 onions, coarsely chopped
3 to 3½ lbs. scallops of veal, or cubed veal stew meat
3 tablespoons butter
1½ tablespoons paprika
½ cup dry white wine
¾ cup chicken broth
1 teaspoon salt
⅛ teaspoon pepper
½ pint sour cream, at room temperature to prevent curdling

Sauté onions in butter until just lightly golden. Cover and cook over low heat until onions are soft, about 30 minutes. Add veal, cover, and simmer until meat is tender, about 45 minutes. Add paprika, wine, stir in well, then simmer another 5 minutes. Remove meat and stir vigorously to purée onions, or run through blender. Return to pot, adding broth if there is not enough sauce, salt and pepper, and cook on low heat until thickened, about 10 minutes. To serve immediately, serve in sour cream, add meat, and heat through.

NOTE: To freeze, combine meat with onion sauce and store. (Do not add sour cream.) When ready to serve, heat on top of stove, then stir in sour cream. Serves 6 to 8.

VEAL IN CHERRY SAUCE*

3 lbs. veal scallops
3 tablespoons vegetable shortening
1 teaspoon salt
½ teaspoon onion powder
1 cup canned cherries
½ cup orange juice
3 tablespoons sherry
¼ teaspoon dry mustard
¼ teaspoon ground ginger
¼ cup sour cream, at room temperature to prevent curdling
1 tablespoon grated orange rind

In electric frying pan, at 375°, melt shortening. Season veal with salt and onion powder and brown on both sides. Drain off fat. Meanwhile, in saucepan over low heat, gently blend and heat through cherries mixed with orange juice, wine, dry mustard, and ginger. When hot, pour sauce through strainer over meat and reserve cherries. In covered frying pan, simmer meat in liquid at 220° for 30 minutes or until tender. Shut off heat, stir in sour cream, and gently fold in cherries, sprinkling all with orange rind. Serves 6 to 8.

NOTE: To freeze, proceed as above, folding in cherries and orange rind, but do not stir in sour cream. When ready to serve, heat meat through. Remove from heat and add sour cream, taking care not to mash the cherries which were added before freezing.

LASAGNA*

2 links hot Italian sausage
1 large onion, chopped fine
1 8-oz. can tomato sauce
1 1-lb. 4-oz. can whole tomatoes
1½ teaspoons salt
¼ teaspoon pepper
1 clove garlic, minced
½ teaspoon oregano

5 tablespoons olive oil
1 lb. ground chuck
⅛ teaspoon garlic powder
½ teaspoon salt
⅛ teaspoon pepper
¼ teaspoon oregano
1 egg
2 tablespoons cold water
1 package broad lasagna noodles
½ lb. mozzarella cheese
1 lb. ricotta cheese
½ lb. grated Parmesan cheese

Brown Italian sausage in deep kettle, turning several times, until sausage is evenly brown. Pierce sausage while it cooks so that fats are released. Add onion, and brown. Mash sausage, then add tomato sauce, whole tomatoes, salt, pepper, minced garlic, and oregano. Simmer over low flame for 1 hour. Meanwhile, heat 2 tablespoons oil in separate skillet. Combine ground chuck with garlic powder, salt, pepper, oregano, egg, and cold water. Roll into marble-sized balls, and brown in oil. Add to sauce as it is cooking, making sure the meatballs simmer at least 20 minutes.

In another large kettle, bring to a boil 5 to 6 quarts of water, salted. Add 3 tablespoons olive oil (this will prevent noodles from sticking) and drop noodles in one at a time, allowing a few seconds between each, cooking until tender. Drain and rinse with cold water immediately. Oil 9 x 13 x 3-inch baking pan, or similar casserole, and, beginning with noodles, alternate layers of noodles, sauce, ricotta cheese, mozzarella pieces, and grated Parmesan, repeating until all noodles are used up, and ending with a layer of sauce and Parmesan. Bake at 375° for 15 to 20 minutes. Serves 6 to 8.

NOTE: To freeze, store, assembled but unbaked, in foil-covered baking pan or casserole. When ready to use, bake at 350° until heated through—until edges are bubbly and noodles are slightly golden but top is not dry. If you prefer, freeze sauce only. When ready to use, prepare remaining ingredients, heat sauce, and assemble to serve immediately.

MANICOTTI*

½ lb. sweet Italian sausage
2 eggs
2 lbs. ricotta cheese
1 cup diced mozzarella cheese
½ cup Parmesan cheese
1 1-lb. can prepared pizza sauce
1 12-oz. box ribbed manicotti

Brown sausage in own fat. Mix eggs into ricotta cheese; add diced mozzarella and almost all the Parmesan cheese, reserving some for later. Mash sausage meat and add to mixture. Boil manicotti in salted water, four noodles at a time for 3 minutes each; remove and repeat until all are cooked, making sure not to make them too soft. Pour some pizza sauce on bottom of shallow casserole. Fill cooked noodles with cheese mixture, stuffing from both ends, place side by side in sauce, and cover with remaining sauce and Parmesan cheese. Bake at 350° for 35 minutes. Serves 6.

NOTE: To freeze, store unbaked in a covered casserole. When ready to serve, heat at 325° until cooked through, but not dry, about 45 minutes.

COMPANY FRANKS AND BEANS*

2 lbs. frankfurters (preferably the large ones called specials), cut into 1-inch slices
1 lb. fresh mushrooms, sliced
1 green pepper, cubed
3 tablespoons butter
2 cans condensed tomato soup (undiluted)
3 1-lb. 4-oz. cans baked beans

Sauté frankfurter slices, mushrooms, and pepper in butter, add remaining ingredients, and simmer until hot. Serves 8 to 10.

TUNA CASSEROLE*

1 8-oz. package wide egg noodles
1½ cans cream of mushroom soup
1½ teaspoons salt
½ teaspoon pepper
1 1-lb. 4-oz. can whole tomatoes, drained
2 onions, chopped
1 green pepper
4 tablespoons butter
1 7-oz. can tuna fish, drained
¼ teaspoon thyme
2 cups crushed potato chips

Cook noodles in salted boiling water until tender. Drain and rinse in cold water to stop cooking. Mix mushroom soup with salt and pepper. Drain tomatoes. Sauté onions and green pepper in butter until limp, but still fresh in color. Drain tuna fish. Grease casserole, and beginning with noodles, make alternating layers of noodles, soup, tuna, sautéed vegetables, and tomato, repeating until all is used. Top with thyme and crushed potato chips. Bake uncovered at 350° for 30 minutes. Serves 8 to 10.

NOTE: To freeze, omit potato chips and cover casserole before baking. When ready to use, bake frozen until heated through, at 325° for 60 minutes, topping with potato chips during last 15 minutes.

SHRIMP CREOLE*

3 tablespoons salad oil
1 onion, sliced
1 green pepper, seeded and cut into strips
8 mushrooms, cut in large dices
1 1-lb. 4-oz. can of tomatoes
1 teaspoon salt
4 peppercorns
A few drops of Worcestershire
Pinch of sugar
1 lb. cooked cleaned shrimp

Heat salad oil in skillet, add onion and pepper, and cook until raw look disappears and the vegetables are just shiny. Stir in mushrooms, tomatoes, salt, peppercorns, Worcestershire sauce, and sugar. Cook until most of the liquid evaporates (about 15 minutes). Add shrimp, and cook only long enough to heat through. Served with 2 cups steamed rice. Serves 4.

NOTE: To freeze, transfer shrimp to freezer container. When ready to serve, defrost and reheat in electric skillet at 375° for 5 to 8 minutes until heated through. Steamed rice should be prepared just before ready to serve. If you prefer, you may mix shrimp and cooked rice, and freeze together in covered casserole. To serve, heat frozen casserole at 325° for 45 minutes.

STUFFED CABBAGE*

1 large white cabbage
1 lb. ground chuck
½ onion, chopped fine in blender
½ cup cooked rice
½ teaspoon salt
Pepper to taste
1 1-lb. 13-oz. can tomatoes
1 onion, minced
2 tablespoons vinegar
2 tablespoons sugar
¼ cup dark Karo syrup
20 gingersnaps, crushed

Separate the cabbage into single leaves, keeping each leaf intact. Use only largest leaves—about 10 to 15 in an average head of cabbage. Spread out in a bowl and pour boiling water over them, letting them soak while preparing the filling. Combine ground chuck, onion, rice, and seasonings. Drain the cabbage leaves, which should be somewhat wilted and soft. If center vein is still stiff, cut out in narrow V-shape and overlap the two cut sides. Fill with a spoonful or two of the meat (depending on size of leaf). Fold each in on two sides, then roll up and fasten with toothpick. Place in large kettle or freeze-and-serve pot and cover with tomatoes, onion, vinegar, sugar, and Karo syrup. Add gingersnaps and continue simmering for 1 hour more. Serves 8 to 10.

NOTE: To freeze, transfer to freezer container. If cooked in a freeze-and-serve pot, such as porcelain-enameled iron or a heat resistant casserole which has tight fitting lid, stuffed cabbage may

be frozen when cooled. To serve, heat frozen casserole in 350°
oven for 1¼ hours.

Side Dishes

ORANGE CARROTS*

**2 packages frozen baby carrots or small fresh carrots, with cooking
liquid reserved**
1 orange, cut up, seeded if necessary, and peeled, half the peel reserved
2 tablespoons butter
4 tablespoons sugar
Dash cinnamon and ground allspice

Cook carrots until tender. Combine orange, orange peel, butter,
sugar, spices, and 2 tablespoons of hot liquid in which the carrots
have been cooked, in blender, and blend a few seconds, until
orange peel is finely chopped. Pour over carrots, cool, and freeze
in covered casserole. Heat to serve. Serves 4 to 6.

SPINACH PIE*

2 lbs. fresh spinach, chopped
**½ lb. Phyllo leaves (strudel leaves) (these may be purchased frozen;
defrost to use)**
¼ lb. butter, melted
20 scallions, (2 bunches) sliced into thin circles
¾ lb. feta cheese, crumbled
5 eggs, slightly beaten
½ cup olive oil

On bottom of 9 x 13 x 2-inch baking pan, spread out Phyllo leaves, brushing each leaf with melted butter. Combine remaining ingredients and layer in baking pan alternately with one or two leaves, buttered. Build in this fashion until all spinach has been used, ending with Phyllo leaves, which have been individually buttered. Bake at 400° for 15 minutes, then at 350° for 40 minutes more. Serve hot to 8 to 10.

NOTE: To freeze, cover baking pan with aluminum foil when cool. To serve, bake frozen pan at 350° for 45 minutes.

SWEET-AND-SOUR RED CABBAGE*

1 medium red cabbage, shredded
1 tablespoon salad oil
1 small onion, chopped
1 large apple, peeled and cut into small cubes
½ cup boiling water
4 tablespoons wine vinegar
2 tablespoons brown sugar
1 teaspoon salt

Heat oil in casserole, and add all remaining ingredients. Simmer for 20 minutes, stirring occasionally. Serves 4 to 6.

NOTE: Freeze in casserole. To serve, defrost for about 3 hours, then simmer over low heat until heated through.

GREEN PEA AND MUSHROOM CASSEROLE*

2 packages frozen peas
½ lb. mushrooms, sliced
2 tablespoons butter
2 tablespoons light cream
⅛ teaspoon marjoram
½ teaspoon salt
Dash pepper
1 tablespoon dry sherry
½ cup blanched toasted almond slivers

Cook peas according to package directions. Sauté mushrooms in butter until tender, about 5 minutes. Add cream. Pour over hot peas, add marjoram, salt, pepper, sherry, and stir gently. Top with toasted almonds. Heat through. Serves 4.

MACARONI AND CHEESE*

½ lb. elbow macaroni
4 tablespoons butter
2 teaspoons flour
½ quart milk
1 lb. processed American cheese, cut into strips

Prepare macaroni according to box instructions. Drain and rinse in cold water. In saucepan, melt butter, stir in flour, and when smooth, gradually add milk, stirring until thickened. Add half of the cheese, stirring to distribute evenly. Place macaroni in freeze-and-serve casserole, pour sauce over it, and top with sliced pieces of remaining cheese. Freeze until needed. To serve, place covered casserole in cold oven and bake at 375° for 1¼ hours. Remove cover and continue cooking for 15 minutes more, or until casserole is heated through and top is bubbly and golden brown. Serves 8.

ORZO IN CREAMED MUSHROOM SAUCE*

1 package macaroni rice (orzo)
1 teaspoon salt
⅛ teaspoon pepper
¾ lb. fresh mushrooms
1 medium onion, finely chopped
3 tablespoons butter
½ pint sour cream

Cook orzo according to package directions for firm texture. Season and sauté mushrooms and onion in butter until soft. Remove from heat. Stir in sour cream and combine with orzo. Serves 8 to 10.

NOTE: To freeze, follow above directions, but do not add sour cream. When ready to serve, defrost, heat orzo and mushroom sauce, then add sour cream and toss lightly.

NOODLE PUDDING*

½ lb. broad egg noodles
⅓ cup melted butter
½ cup sugar
½ teaspoon cinnamon
1 teaspoon almond extract
½ cup white raisins
2 apples, peeled and cored and cut in small cubes
½ cup chopped walnuts
2 eggs, beaten
2 tablespoons sugar mixed with ⅛ teaspoon cinnamon

Cook noodles in boiling salted water for 10 minutes. Drain and rinse with cold water. Place noodles in mixing bowl, toss with melted butter, then add the sugar, cinnamon, and almond extract. Mix in gently. Combine raisins, apples, and nuts and stir in noodles. Place in well-greased casserole and pour the beaten eggs over all. Bake in 375° oven for 20 minutes, then sprinkle with the sugar and cinnamon mixture, and continue baking for another 15 to 20 minutes. Serves 8 to 10.

NOTE: When cool, freeze in baking pan covered with foil. To serve, heat frozen pudding at 350° for 1 hour.

RISOTTO*

½ cup olive oil
1 cup rice
1 teaspoon salt
¼ teaspoon pepper
2 cups boiling water
A few threads of saffron, soaked in 1 tablespoon water
1 egg, beaten
4 tablespoons grated Romano or Parmesan cheese

In a large saucepan, heat olive oil. Add rice and cook over medium heat until rice is glossy and lightly golden. Add salt and pepper and pour in 2 cups of boiling water. Add saffron liquid and stir in. Cover and simmer for 30 minutes, or until water is absorbed and rice is soft. Stir in beaten raw egg and grated cheese. Cool and freeze, covered, ready to serve. Serves 4 to 5.

NOTE: When ready to serve, defrost and reheat in 2 tablespoons oil in large saucepan, stirring constantly until steaming hot.

HOT FRUIT COMPOTE*

1 1-lb. can sliced pineapple
½ lb. dried apricots
½ lb. dried prunes
1 1-lb. can peach halves
1 1-lb. can pear halves
1 1-lb. can black cherries, pitted, if available
1 pint jar applesauce
Juice of 1 lemon
4 tablespoons brown sugar

Drain off all juices, saving only the pineapple juice. Marinate apricots and prunes in the pineapple juice for 1 hour. Drain marinade and save. Mix all fruits, sprinkle with lemon juice and some of the pineapple juice. Grease baking dish. Pour in all the fruits, distribute so that arrangement is attractive, and top with a sprinkling of brown sugar. Bake in 350° oven for 1 hour. Use as an accompaniment to ham, pot roast, or poultry dishes. Serves 8 to 10.

NOTE: Freeze in heat-and-serve platter, covered with foil. To serve, heat covered frozen platter at 350° for 1 hour.

PRUNE AND APPLE BAKE*

1 lb. almonds, whole, skinned
1½ lbs. dried prunes, cooked and pitted
2 cans sliced apples
1 cup golden raisins
½ lb. margarine
Salt and pepper to taste

Mix together all ingredients, cutting the margarine in to distribute evenly. Season lightly with salt and pepper. Bake in shallow pan until thoroughly heated and bubbling, about ½ hour. Use as accompaniment for potted meat dishes or poultry. Serves 6 to 8.

NOTE: Freeze in heat-and-serve platter, covered with foil. To serve, heat covered frozen platter at 350° for 1 hour.

BUTTER CRESCENT ROLLS*

1 cup milk
½ cup shortening
1 package dry, granulated yeast, dissolved in ¼ cup lukewarm water
½ cup sugar
3 eggs, slightly beaten
1 teaspoon salt
4 cups all-purpose flour
¼ cup butter, melted

Scald milk and remove from heat. Add shortening. Allow to cool to lukewarm. Combine dissolved yeast with sugar and add to luke-warm milk mixture. Add eggs, salt, and stir in flour, mixing well. Place in warm place, covered with clean kitchen towel, and let rise until double in bulk (about 2 to 3 hours). Place on floured surface, divide in three sections, and roll each section into a circle about ½ inch thick. Brush with melted butter and cut into narrow pie-shaped wedges. Roll each section, starting at the broadest point. Place on greased pan, pointed end down. Let rise in warm place until double in size. Bake for 10 minutes in preheated oven at 400°. Makes 45 to 48 rolls.

NOTE: Freeze cooled rolls in baking pan, covered with foil or plastic wrap. To serve, bake in preheated oven until heated through and crescents turn golden brown and lightly crisped on top.

OATMEAL BREAD*

1½ cups boiling water
1 cup uncooked oatmeal
⅓ cup shortening
½ cup light molasses
1 tablespoon salt
2 cakes or two packages dry granulated yeast, dissolved in ½ cup warm water
2 eggs
5½ cups sifted all-purpose flour

Combine boiling water with oats, shortening, molasses, and salt. Add dissolved yeast and mix well. Blend in eggs and gradually add flour, mixing until well blended. Place dough in greased bowl and cover. Store in refrigerator at least 2 hours. Shape into 2 loaves and place in greased 9 x 5 x 3-inch loaf pans. Cover and let rise in warm place until double in bulk, about 2 to 3 hours. Bake at 350° for 1 hour. Makes two loaves of bread.

NOTE: When cool wrap in aluminum foil and freeze until ready to use. To serve, defrost at room temperature for ½ hour or heat in 325° oven for 20 minutes.

HERB-GARLIC FRENCH BREAD*

1 loaf French bread
¼ cup butter
½ teaspoon garlic powder
½ cup chopped green onions or sweet onions, including some of tops
2 tablespoons parsley flakes
2 tablespoons prepared mustard
2 tablespoons sesame seeds or poppy seeds

Split bread lengthwise. Cream butter. Blend in garlic, onion, and parsley. Spread split loaf with butter mixture. Spread with prepared mustard. Top with sesame seeds or poppy seeds. Cut bread diagonally in 1½-inch slices not quite through the bottom crust. Heat in a 350° oven for about 12 minutes or until lightly browned. Hard rolls may be used instead of bread. Serves 12 to 14.

NOTE: To freeze, prepare bread as above, with spreads and seeds. Wrap tightly in aluminum foil and freeze. When ready to serve, heat frozen loaf in 350° oven for 20 minutes.

Desserts

CHEESE-FILLED PANCAKES WITH FRUIT*

3 eggs
½ teaspoon salt
1 cup milk
1 cup all-purpose flour
2 cups farmer or cottage cheese
2 tablespoons sugar
¾ cup chopped maraschino cheeries and canned crushed pineapple, mixed

Beat eggs slightly, add salt. Add milk and flour. The batter should be thin. Heat small (6-inch) skillet and grease lightly by rubbing shortening around full surface and sides with paper towel. Spoon 2 tablespoons of batter into pan, and tilt to distribute evenly. For thin pancakes, pour off excess batter. Cook over moderate heat until edges curl away from sides. Turn out on clean cloth with cooked side up. Continue until all batter is used up. Mix together well cheese, sugar, and the remaining egg. Add fruit which has been well drained. Place a spoonful of the filling on each pancake.

Fold in from each side, then roll over from third side towards the fourth. Place in flat container, cover, and freeze. To serve, place pancakes in pan with hot butter, and cook on low flames, to allow slow defrosting. When pancake softens and begins to turn golden, turn over gently so as not to break open, and fry until golden on the other side. Pancakes may also be heated in larger quantity if placed in buttered pan and brushed with melted butter and heated in 350° oven for 30 minutes. Preparation time may be shortened if pancakes are defrosted prior to frying, which is the preferred method of heating. Serves 6 to 8.

RUSSIAN BREAD*

3 eggs
1 cup sugar
1 tablespoon sour cream
½ lb. butter
4 cups all-purpose flour
¼ teaspoon baking powder
¼ lb. blanched cut almonds
Raspberry preserves

Beat eggs with sugar, add sour cream, and cream in butter. Combine flour with baking powder and sift gradually into mixture. Refrigerate dough for several hours, or freeze for ½ hour. Divide into sections and make sausage lengths. Freeze until needed, wrapping individually in aluminum foil or plastic wrap. To use, defrost, roll out flat, and spread with preserves and almonds. Roll up. Bake at 350° for 20 to 25 minutes, or until golden brown. Remove from oven, cool slightly, cut into slices, and return to warm oven to dry out. Yields 50 to 60 slices.

NOTE: Store in freezer in covered container to use as needed. To serve, defrost at room temperature for about an hour. Heat, if desired.

JAM COOKIES*

4 cups flour
½ lb. butter
3 eggs, separated
2 tablespoons sugar
½ pint sour cream
Pinch of salt
1 jar jam
1 cup crushed walnuts mixed with 1 tablespoon sugar (use blender)

Pile flour on flat surface, and cut in butter and 2 egg yolks (reserving whites) to make crumbs. Mix sugar with sour cream and remaining egg yolk and add to flour mixture. Make a ball of dough and roll out on floured surface. Cut out circles with a water glass. When all dough is used up, cut out small circles inside one-half the cut cookies, using a timble or similar small container with sharp lip. Place a dot of jam in the center of each complete circle. Dip each donutlike cut-out circle in egg white and crushed nuts mixed with sugar. Place over jam-dotted circle, nut-side-up. Bake at 350° for 25 to 30 minutes. Makes 30 to 40 cookies, depending on size of circle.

NOTE: Wrap to freeze. When ready to serve, defrost at room temperature for about ½ hour, or heat in 350° oven for 5 minutes.

CANDIED COOKIES*

1 cup butter
1 cup sifted confectioners' sugar
1 egg
2½ cups all-purpose flour
¼ teaspoon cream of tartar
½ cup chopped pecans
½ cup chopped candied fruit
1 cup whole candied cherries

Cream butter and sugar, beat in egg. Stir in dry ingredients. Blend in nuts, fruit, and cherries. Form into rolls 1½ inches thick. Wrap in plastic wrap and freeze. To use, heat oven to 375°. Slice rolls very thinly, place on greased baking sheet, and bake 6 to 8 minutes. Makes 10 dozen.

NOTE: Wrap to freeze. When ready to serve defrost at room temperature for about ½ hour, or heat in 350° oven for 10 minutes.

PECAN STRIPS*

¼ lb. sweet butter
1 egg yolk
1 cup sugar
2 cups flour
1 teaspoon almond extract
1 teaspoon vanilla extract
12 oz. pecans, ground in blender

Cream butter with egg yolk; beat in sugar. Sift in flour and beat until smooth. Add extracts and ground pecans. Shape into long rolls, about 2 inches in diameter. Cut into ½-inch strips and place on ungreased cookie sheet, forming into crescents. Bake 10 to 12 minutes at 350°. Makes 5 dozen.

NOTE: Wrap to freeze. When ready to serve, defrost at room temperature for about ½ hour, or heat in 350° oven for 5 minutes.

COFFEE CAKE*

¼ lb. butter
1 cup sugar
2 eggs
2 cups all-purpose flour
1 teaspoon baking soda
1 teaspoon baking powder
1 cup sour cream
1 teaspoon vanilla

TOPPING

½ cup broken walnuts
⅓ cup sugar
2 teaspoons cinnamon

Cream butter, sugar, and eggs. Sift dry ingredients. Add alternately dry ingredients and sour cream to butter mixture. Add vanilla. Put half of batter in greased spring-form pan or ring mold. Distribute half the topping mix over the batter, then add remaining batter and cover with rest of topping. Bake 40 minutes at 370° or until wooden toothpick inserted in middle comes out clean. May be heated to serve 10 to 12.

NOTE: Freeze intact when cool, wrapped in aluminum foil. When ready to serve, defrost at room temperature for at least 1 hour, or reheat in 350° oven for 20 minutes.

NUT TORTE WITH ORANGE FILLING*

4 eggs, separated
1 cup sugar
2 tablespoons flour
½ teaspoon salt
½ teaspoon baking powder
1 tablespoon orange juice or 1 tablespoon rum
2 cups blender-grated pecans

FILLING

½ cup heavy cream
1½ teaspoons grated orange rind

FROSTING

1 6-oz. pack semisweet chocolate bits
½ cup sour cream
Dash of salt

Beat egg yolks until thick, add sugar, and beat until light and fluffy. Mix flour, salt, and baking powder and stir in. Add juice or rum and grated nuts. Beat egg whites until stiff and gently fold in. Pour into two 8-inch layer pans which are well greased and lined with wax paper. Bake at 350° for 25 minutes, or until touching gently leaves no dent. Cool. Remove from pans. One to three hours before serving, put layers together with heavy cream, whipped and flavored with orange rind. Top with frosting.

To prepare frosting, melt semisweet chocolate bits in double boiler over hot water. Stir in sour cream and salt. Mix, spread, and garnish with nut halves.

NOTE: Freeze uncovered torte until icing is hard. Wrap in aluminum foil until needed. When ready to serve, uncover and defrost at room temperature, about 1 hour.

WALNUT SOUR CREAM CAKE*

1 cup butter
1 cup sugar
2 eggs
1 teaspoon vanilla
2 cups sifted flour
1 teaspoon baking powder
1 teaspoon baking soda
½ teaspoon salt
1 cup sour cream

FILLING AND TOPPING

⅓ cup brown sugar
¼ cup granulated sugar
1 teaspoon cinnamon
1 cup chopped walnuts

Cream butter and sugar until fluffy. Add eggs and vanilla and beat well. Add dry ingredients and sour cream, a third at a time, beating well after each addition. Beat until smooth. Spread half the batter in a well-greased and floured 9 x 12 x 2-inch pan. Sprinkle batter with one-half the filling. Spread on the remaining batter and sprinkle with the remaining topping. Bake at 350° for 35 minutes or until knife comes out clean when inserted into the center of the cake.

NOTE: Freeze wrapped in aluminum foil. To serve, defrost at room temperature, about 1 hour, or reheat in 350° oven for 20 minutes.

ALMOND COFFEE CAKE*

3 tablespoons sugar
1 package active dry yeast
½ cup warm water
½ lb. butter
1 teaspoon salt
2½ cups flour
3 eggs, separated
¾ cup sugar
1 teaspoon vanilla
⅔ lb. almond paste, or 1 can almond cake-and-pastry filling

Combine sugar with yeast and warm water. Stir and allow to foam. Cream together butter, salt, and flour, add egg yolks, and yeast mixture. Mix and place in covered bowl overnight in refrigerator. When ready to bake, beat egg whites with sugar and vanilla until meringue is formed. Divide dough into two parts. Roll each flat, ¼ inch thick, and spread each with almond paste topped with meringue. Reserve some of the meringue for topping. Roll up dough in jelly-roll fashion. Place in 9-inch greased tube pans, with ends overlapping. Spread reserved meringue over top of each cake. Bake at 350° for 1 hour. Yields 2 coffee cakes, serving 8 to 10 each.

NOTE: Freeze in aluminum foil until ready to serve. Heat to serve at 350° for 25 minutes.

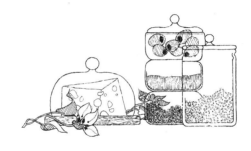

YEAST CAKE*

2 oz. compressed yeast
½ cup warm water
½ lb. butter
3 cups flour
1 egg and 2 egg yolks (reserve whites)
3 tablespoons sour cream
6 tablespoons sugar
Cinnamon, raisins, nuts, or jam, according to your preference

Crumble yeast into warm water, cover with foil, and let stand while preparing dough. Blend butter and flour on medium speed, add whole egg and egg yolks, sour cream, and cream together. Add yeast mixture. Refrigerate overnight, to rise, covered with dish towel. When ready to bake, divide dough into 2 parts. Roll each into ¼-inch thickness. Beat egg whites with sugar until glossy and stiff. Spread dough with meringue and add nuts, cinnamon, raisins, or jam. Repeat with second half of dough. Roll up dough in jelly-roll fashion. Place in 9-inch greased tube pans, with ends overlapping. Cover and let rise in warm place for at least 2 hours. Bake at 350° for 45 minutes, or until wooden toothpick inserted in middle comes out clean. Heat to serve. Serves 10.

NOTE: Freeze in aluminum foil until ready to serve. Defrost at room temperature for about 1 hour, or reheat in 350° oven for about 20 minutes.

CREAM CHEESE TARTS*

4 oz. sweet butter, room temperature
4 oz. cream cheese, room temperature
1 cup all-purpose flour

Mix butter and cheese, sift in flour, and mix until well distributed. Cover with waxed paper and chill in freezer for 1 hour, or refrigerate overnight.

NOTE: You may store dough in freezer for several months and bake when needed or complete the baking of assembled tarts and then freeze until ready to serve. When ready to serve, defrost at room temperature for 45 minutes.

FILLING

2 eggs
1 8-oz. package cream cheese
½ cup sugar
1½ tablespoons flour
2 teaspoons vanilla
⅛ teaspoon salt
½ cup sour cream

Combine all ingredients except sour cream. Beat until smooth. Blend in sour cream and fill tarts.

To prepare tarts, roll out dough until thin, but not translucent. Cut into circles somewhat larger than top diameter of 2-inch tart shell. Fit dough in shell, pressing onto sides. Trim top. Fill half full and bake at 325° for 25 minutes, or until cheese mixture looks dry in center. Turn oven off and leave in for additional cooling, which prevents the filling from falling.

NOTE: Tarts may be frozen when cool, but should not be glazed until ready to serve. Glaze (see p. 152) when defrosted at room temperature for about ½ hour.

GLAZE

1 package frozen strawberries, defrosted
1½ teaspoons cornstarch
16 large fresh strawberries

Drain juice off strawberries, and stir cornstarch into juice. Cook over low heat, stirring until clear and thick. Mix in frozen strawberries and add red food coloring, if desired. Arrange whole fresh strawberries (one large one is usually sufficient for each) on top of the tarts, and pour the cooked strawberry mix over them. Makes 14 to 16 tarts.

FUDGE BROWNIES*

¼ lb. butter
3 squares bitter-sweet baking chocolate
3 eggs
1 cup sugar
1½ cups chopped walnuts
½ cup flour
1 teaspoon vanilla

Melt together butter and chocolate squares. Cream together eggs with sugar, beating very well. Combine chocolate mixture with egg mixture. Add nuts, flour, and vanilla, and stir in until well distributed. Spread in 9 x 13 x 3-inch buttered pan. Bake at 350° for 25 to 30 minutes, until just done. Do not overbake. Frost immediately, while hot (see p. 153).

FROSTING

1 cup confectioners' sugar
1 square baking chocolate, melted
1 tablespoon butter
1 teaspoon vanilla
2 tablespoons hot strong coffee

Beat above ingredients together with mixer. Spread over top of brownies while they are still in the pan. Cut into squares when cool to make 3 dozen brownies.

NOTE: Freeze uncovered, until icing is hard. Store in plastic container. To serve, defrost at room temperature, about 1 hour.

POUND CAKE*

1½ cups flour
1½ cups sugar
¼ teaspoon baking soda
½ lb. sweet butter, room temperature
5 large eggs, separated
1 teaspoon cream of tartar
Pinch of salt
1½ teaspoons vanilla
1½ teaspoons lemon juice

Sift flour with baking soda and half the sugar into large bowl. Add softened butter and work into the flour by hand, plastering it against the bowl in a steady motion, gathering as much of the dough at one time as possible. Continue beating against the bowl until smooth. Separate the eggs. If possible, leave the individual yolks separated in the shell, or add one yolk at a time to the flour and butter mixture, kneading in until all yolks are used. Beat whites with mixer until peaked but not dry. Add rest of sugar gradually while continuing to use the mixer. Stop the mixer and fold in the cream of tartar and salt gently, using a fork or your hand, with fingers separated. Add vanilla and lemon juice to first mixture, then fold in egg whites with fork or by hand, with fingers separated. Batter will be lumpy at first, but will smooth out as you continue. Pour into greased and floured tube pan and bake in preheated oven at 350° for 1 hour. DO NOT OPEN OVEN WHILE BAKING. Shut off oven but leave cake in for 10 minutes longer. Remove from oven and leave in pan 10 minutes longer; then turn out. Serves 12 to 14.

NOTE: Freeze wrapped in aluminum foil or cut into portions and wrap each slice individually. Defrost whole cake at room temperature for about 1 hour; individual slices for about 10 minutes.

SEVEN-LAYER CAKE*

ICING

1 6-oz. package of semisweet chocolate chips
3 whole eggs and 1 egg yolk
¾ cup sugar, scant
1 tablespoon flour
¼ cup milk
¾ lb. sweet butter, creamed
1 teaspoon vanilla

PASTRY

6 eggs, separated, and one egg white (left from icing ingredients)
¾ cup sugar
1 cup all-purpose flour

Begin by preparing the icing. Melt chocolate chips in saucepan over low flame. Place eggs and egg yolk in double boiler, add sugar mixed with flour, milk, and heat, stirring constantly. When thick, add melted chocolate. Cool mixture to lukewarm. Then beat in creamed butter and vanilla. To prepare batter, beat egg yolks with sugar until lemon colored. Sift in flour and blend. Beat 7 egg whites until they stand in peaks but are not dry. Fold whites into yolk mixture. Grease and flour 2 flat cookie sheets with no edges, if available. If not, use standard cookie pans upside-down, greasing and flouring the underside. Spread batter thickly over the complete surface, using all the batter for the 2 pans. Bake in 350° oven for 8 to 10 minutes. Watch carefully so that the edges do not become too crisp. Remove from oven and immediately loosen the edges with a spatula. Cut each sheet lengthwise into 3 strips, and remove as needed. Spread chocolate icing evenly on first strip of pastry, place second strip on top, ice again, add another strip, and continue in this manner until all strips have been used. Ice top and sides of cake, and, if desired, decorate with slivered almonds.

NOTE: Freeze whole or in thinly sliced sections, wrapping after icing has frozen. To serve, remove from freezer at onset of dinner. It should be served cooler than room temperature. If you prefer, icing may be prepared much earlier (it will keep for months) and frozen, as may the leftover egg white. Both will need to be completely defrosted before being used for the layers of cake. If icing has already been frozen, however, it would be preferable not to freeze the completed cake but rather to keep it refrigerated (which may be done for several days), covering it after it is cold and firm. Remove from refrigerator ½ hour before serving, slicing while it is still firm. Serves 12 to 14.

CHOCOLATE ROLL*

4 eggs, separated
¾ cup sugar
2 tablespoons cold water
1 teaspoon vanilla
½ cup flour
¼ cup cocoa
2 tablespoons cornstarch
1 teaspoon baking powder
Dash salt
½ cup confectioners' sugar, sifted
1 pint heavy sweet cream, whipped

Beat egg whites, slowly adding half of the sugar. Beat egg yolks in water; add rest of sugar and vanilla. Carefully fold yolks into whites. Sift flour, cocoa, cornstarch, baking powder, and salt. Fold into egg mixture with whisk. Grease jelly-roll pan, 10 x 15 x ¼ inches, line with brown paper, and grease paper. Spread batter in pan. Slash with knife to prevent air bubbles. Bake at 375° for 15 minutes. Leave in pan, trim off crisp edges, and turn out onto dish towel which has been sprinkled liberally with confectioners' sugar. Roll towel and cake lengthwise, keeping rolled up until cool. When ready to serve, unroll, fill with whipped cream and roll up again.

ICING

2 squares baking chocolate
1½ teaspoons butter
1 egg
1 cup confectioners' sugar
½ teaspoon vanilla
¼ cup heavy cream, whipped

Melt chocolate and butter over low flame. Beat egg, add confectioners' sugar and vanilla. Beat until light, add chocolate mixture, and cream together. Cool. Fold in whipped cream and ice. Serves 12.

NOTE: Freeze uncovered until icing is hard. Wrap. To serve, defrost in refrigerator for 3 hours.

OPEN APPLE PIE*

1 9-inch unbaked pie shell (see p. 89)
10 cups pared and quartered green sour cooking apples
1 cup sugar
4 tablespoons enriched flour
1 teaspoon salt
⅓ cup light sweet cream
¼ cup milk
⅛ teaspoon cinnamon

Fill unbaked shell with apples. Combine sugar, flour, and salt. Add cream and milk, and beat. Pour mixture over apples, and sprinkle with the cinnamon. Bake at 375° for 1½ hours, or until apples are soft but still retain their shape. (For first hour of baking, cover pie lightly with aluminum foil, then uncover to complete baking.) Serve warm, with slices of cheddar cheese. Serves 8 to 10.

NOTE: Wrap and freeze, omitting cheese. To serve, heat in 350° oven for 35 minutes. Add cheese slices to decorate before bringing to table.

COCONUT ICE CREAM PIE*

2 egg whites, unbeaten
⅛ teaspoon cream of tartar
Dash of salt
½ cup sugar
½ teaspoon vanilla
1 cup flaked coconut

Combine egg whites, cream of tartar, and salt in mixing bowl. Beat until foamy. Add sugar, 2 tablespoons at a time, beating after each addition until sugar is well blended. Continue beating until mixture is very stiff. Fold in vanilla and coconut. Spread mixture on bottom and sides of lightly greased 9-inch pie pan. Bake at 325° for about 30 minutes, or until shell feels dry and firm. Cool. Fill shell with ice cream. Serves 8 to 10.

NOTE: Freeze, wrapped, until ready to serve. Do not defrost before serving.

KEY LIME PIE*

1 10-inch baked graham cracker pie crust (see p. 57)
4 eggs, separated
1 can sweetened condensed milk
½ cup fresh lime juice (if not available, bottled may be used)
4 tablespoons confectioners' sugar
A few drops of green food coloring
½ cup heavy cream, whipped

Mix egg yolks with condensed milk. Fold in lime juice. Beat egg whites, gradually adding confectioners' sugar and continue beating until stiff. Gently fold beaten egg whites into other mixture and add food coloring until pleasing green color is attained. Pour into cooled graham cracker crust and bake for 10 minutes at 300°. Cool and freeze until ready to serve. May be served just a few minutes after taking out of freezer. It is preferable not to garnish with the whipped cream until ready to serve. Serves 8 to 10.

FROZEN PUMPKIN SQUARES*

½ cup orange juice
4 tablespoons sugar
1 egg, separated
⅓ cup brown sugar
1 teaspoon cinnamon
¼ teaspoon ginger
¼ teaspoon nutmeg
⅛ teaspoon ground cloves
¾ cup cooked (or canned) pumpkin
12 gingersnaps
1 cup heavy cream, whipped

Combine orange juice, sugar, and egg yolk in top of double boiler and cook over low flame until slightly thickened. Add brown sugar, spices, and pumpkin. Stir until sugar is dissolved. Beat egg white until it forms peaks but is still moist, and fold into pumpkin mixture. Crush gingersnaps and scatter half in bottom of tray. Fold whipped cream into pumpkin mixture and pour into crumb-lined tray. Sprinkle the remaining crumbs on top of pumpkin. Freeze quickly. Cut into squares. Serves 8.

NOTE: Do not defrost to serve.

PARFAITS*

3 tablespoons shredded coconut
½ cup mixed, diced, candied fruit
1 tablespoon maraschino cherry juice
2 tablespoons orange juice
1 egg yolk
1 cup sugar
1 cup heavy cream, whipped
1 additional cup heavy cream

Soak coconut and candied fruit in maraschino juice and orange juice. Beat egg yolk with sugar until thick and lemon colored. Whip heavy cream and fold lightly into egg mixture. Pour into any flat baking pan with sides, and freeze until firm. Mixture never becomes very hard because it is so rich. Serve in parfait glasses with alternating layers of whipped cream. Serves 6 to 8.

NOTE: Serve frozen.

EGYPTIAN ICE CREAM*

2 quarts vanilla ice cream
1 pint heavy cream, whipped
24 ladyfingers
½ cup rum
2 cups sliced canned peaches, or fresh strawberries, sliced and sweetened to taste

Cut each quart of ice cream in half. (Brick ice cream is easier to work with.) Allow to soften just enough so that it can be easily molded. Spread one of the halves on a large platter, shaping ice cream into a rectangle about 12 x 4 inches. Mix another half quart with the whipped cream, blending well. Spread 12 ladyfingers, split, over ice cream rectangle, and sprinkle with half the rum. Cover ladyfingers with one-half the fruit and top these with half of the whipped cream mixture. Top with another half quart of ice cream, and proceed to build another layer of ladyfingers sprinkled with remaining rum, topping this with remaining fruit and whipped cream mixture, and ending with remaining half quart of ice cream, as above. You will have to work fast, and may prefer to do this in stages, freezing mold after each addition of the whipped cream mixture. If so, ice cream not being used immediately should be kept in freezer and removed in portions as needed. When mold is fully assembled, freeze until firm. Garnish with fresh strawberries and fresh mint leaves. Slice at the table. Serves 12 to 14.

NOTE: Serve frozen.

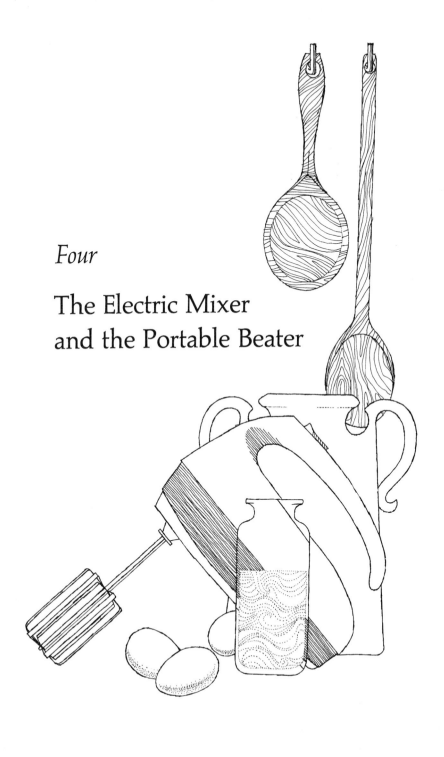

Four

The Electric Mixer
and the Portable Beater

The Electric Mixer
and the Portable Beater

THE ELECTRIC MIXER is so well established as an essential piece of equipment in the modern kitchen that its inclusion in this book may seem strange to some readers. Of course, you use your mixer for making cakes and cookies; beating egg whites for soufflés, chiffon pies, and meringues; whipping potatoes and other puréed vegetables; and whipping cream. But if you take a fresh look at this appliance and its attachments, you may very well find that you are not using it nearly as often as you could to make meals more interesting and easier to prepare. For example, you can make delicious and unusual cheese spreads for appetizers and mix in chopped nuts, olives, or clams to add interesting variations in taste and texture. Because the mixer or beater combines ingredients without homogenizing them as does the blender, it is often the right choice for appetizer spreads. Also, when you use the meat grinding attachment of your mixer, you'll find that such unusual dishes as dill-flavored Chicken Cutlets and Russian Meat Pie can be prepared in a matter of minutes.

In this chapter I've attempted to show how your mixer or portable beater can be utilized to create a wide variety of appetizers, main dishes, and side dishes; but perhaps the main emphasis is on start-from-scratch desserts and cakes that have rich, home-cooked flavor no prepackaged mix can approach. Surprise your family or friends with old-fashioned Double Chocolate Layer Cake or Butterscotch Chewy Cake and you'll see that a small amount of extra effort pays great dividends. And at your next dinner party serve Orange Meringue Pie for an unusual and delightful finish.

A word on whether to choose a mixer or portable beater if you're just starting out. The mixer is the best choice if you have a large kitchen and a comfortable amount of storage space; with its attachments, it can serve a variety of functions. In line with my thinking of the kitchen as a laboratory, I even prefer to leave the mixer, as most of the other appliances, out in the open. This is not inconsistent with also liking a neat kitchen, nor does having these mechanical helpers on hand result in the same chaos as having five helping daughters underfoot. I need not wish it on you, but I wouldn't know how to cook any other way!

Portable electric beaters, on the other hand, are cheaper and easier to store and, since they can do most of the same things a mixer can, are a wise choice for apartment dwellers.

Appetizers

SHRIMP PASTE*

1 lb. shrimp
½ cup butter
Salt, celery salt, and cayenne pepper to taste

Boil fresh shrimp for 5 minutes. Shell and clean. Force through food grinding attachment of mixer (blender may be used also). In electric mixer, cream butter, shrimp, and seasonings. Mix until smooth, and pack into 4 x 8 x 3-inch loaf pan. Bake at 350° for 30 minutes, or until mixture leaves the sides of the pan. Cool, then chill before slicing. Serve on crackers or in sliced portions. Serves 6 to 8.

FILLED EDAM

1 round Edam cheese
½ cup light cream

Leave cheese at room temperature. Cut slice off top of cheese. Scoop out center, leaving ¼-inch wall. Scallop edge of cheese shell, using a biscuit cutter as a guide. Whip the cheese with electric mixer, beating in the light cream to make mixture of spreading consistency. Mound the cheese in shell. Store in refrigerator, but remove and leave at room temperature 1 hour before serving with crackers or celery sticks. Serves 8 to 10.

WALNUT SPREAD

1 8-oz. package cream cheese, room temperature
3 tablespoons butter, room temperature
3 tablespoons anchovy butter
½ cup walnut meats, broken into small pieces

With electric beater, whip cheese and add butter and anchovy paste. Stir in walnut meats and serve with chips or crackers.

OLIVE-CHEESE NUGGETS*

½ lb. sharp Cheddar cheese
½ cup butter, soft
1½ cups flour
¼ teaspoon salt
1 teaspoon paprika
Dash of cayenne
About 60 stuffed green olives

Shred cheese and place in mixer with butter. Blend. Sift in dry ingredients and beat until dough is well blended. Drain olives. Use 1 tablespoon of dough for each nugget, and form it around an olive. Continue until all dough is used. Chill at least 30 minutes in refrigerator. Bake at 400° on ungreased cookie sheet for 12 to 15 minutes. Serve hot. Yields 60.

NOTE: May be frozen before baking, or dough may be frozen separately and used as needed.

CLAM AND CHEESE PIE*

1 8-oz. package cream cheese
4 eggs, separated
2 7-oz. cans minced clams, drained
1 teaspoon grated onion
¼ teaspoon Tabasco sauce
Dash of salt
1 9-inch pie pastry, partly baked (see p. 89)

In large bowl of mixer, cream the cheese until very soft. Beat in egg yolks. Add the clams, onion, Tabasco sauce, and salt. Rinse beaters. In small mixer bowl, beat egg whites until stiff and almost dry and fold into cheese mixture. Pour into the pastry shell and bake at 400° until crust is golden and center is just set, about 30 to 35 minutes. Let stand 5 minutes before cutting into wedges to serve hot. Serves 8 to 10.

SWEDISH MEATBALLS*

1 lb. chuck
½ lb. veal
¼ lb. pork
3 slices white bread, with crust removed and torn into soft crumbs
¼ cup cold milk
½ cup chopped onion
2 tablespoons butter
1 cup light cream
¼ cup finely chopped parsley
1 teaspoon salt
1 teaspoon monosodium glutamate
¼ teaspoon ginger
Dash pepper
2 tablespoons butter
1 tablespoon flour
1 can cream of mushroom soup
1 teaspoon dry instant coffee
1 beef bouillon cube, softened in ¼ cup water

Using meat grinding attachment, grind combined meats twice. Soak bread in milk for about 5 minutes. Heat electric skillet and cook onion in 2 tablespoons of butter until tender and glossy. Combine meats, bread mixture, onion, light cream, and seasonings. Beat in electric mixer at medium speed for at least 5 minutes, or until mixture is very light and fluffy. Mixture will be soft. With wet hands, form 1-inch balls. Brown lightly in electric skillet in 2 tablespoons butter, shaking skillet to keep balls round. Continue browning balls, making sure not to crowd them, until all meat is used. Remove meatballs. Stir flour into drippings in fry pan. Add undiluted cream of mushroom soup, coffee, and softened bouillon cube. Heat and stir until gravy is well blended. Return meatballs to gravy and let simmer, uncovered, for about 10 minutes. If thinner gravy is desired, add milk or light cream. Serve hot with toast points or on a bed of noodles. Serves 10.

NOTE: If desired, you may roll 2-inch meatballs and serve as main course. Serves 4 to 6.

Main Dishes

BAKED CHICKEN IN CRUSTY PASTRY

1 3 to 3½ lb. frying chicken, cut up
½ cup flour
2 teaspoons salt
¼ teaspoon pepper
¼ teaspoon paprika
½ cup shortening

Combine flour and seasonings in brown paper bag and toss chicken pieces in mixture until evenly coated. Brown in shortening. Place in baking pan, at least 3 inches deep, which may be used for serving at the table directly from the oven. Leave uncovered. Prepare batter.

BATTER

3 eggs
1½ cups milk
1 cup all-purpose flour, added gradually
1 teaspoon double-acting baking powder
1 teaspoon salt
¼ cup chopped parsley
Drippings from pan in which chicken has been browned

Place all ingredients in mixer bowl and beat together. Pour mixture over chicken in baking dish. Bake at 350° for 1 hour. Serves 5 to 6.

CHICKEN WITH DUMPLINGS

1 2½-lb. frying chicken, cut up
3 cups water
1 onion, chopped
½ bay leaf
2 slices lemon
Salt and pepper to taste

Combine all ingredients, bring to boil, lower heat, and simmer for 35 minutes, or until tender. Remove bay leaf and lemon.

DUMPLINGS

1 cup all-purpose flour, sifted
1 teaspoon baking powder
¾ teaspoon salt
⅛ teaspoon nutmeg
1 teaspoon minced onion
2 egg yolks
⅓ cup milk

Sift together dry ingredients. Add onion. With electric mixer, beat egg yolks with milk, then gradually add dry ingredients and mix until blended. When chicken has simmered for 35 minutes, drop dumpling batter on top of chicken with teaspoon. Cover lightly and simmer 15 minutes, without uncovering. Serve at once. Serves 4.

CHICKEN CHEESE-AND-RICE SOUFFLÉ

WHITE SAUCE

2 tablespoons butter
2 tablespoons flour
1 cup milk
¼ teaspoon salt
⅛ teaspoon paprika

Melt butter, then stir in flour, blending to a smooth paste. Add milk gradually, stirring constantly. Let mixture come to a boil and simmer a few minutes. Add seasonings.

SOUFFLÉ

½ lb. sharp Cheddar cheese, grated in blender
½ teaspoon dry mustard
Salt and pepper to taste
4 eggs, separated
½ can condensed tomato soup
¾ cup cooked rice
1 cup diced cooked chicken

To the hot white sauce, add the grated cheese, mustard, salt, and pepper. Stir until cheese is just melted. Beat in egg yolks, add tomato soup, rice, and chicken. With electric mixer, beat egg whites until they form soft peaks, but are not dry. Fold into chicken mixture very gently to keep in as much air as possible. Pour into greased baking dish with straight sides, and bake at 350° 45 to 50 minutes. Do not open oven door while baking or soufflé will fall. Serves 6.

CHICKEN CUTLETS*

4 whole chicken breasts, boned
¾ lb. veal, boneless
2 pork chops, boned
2 eggs, beaten
6 slices white bread, crusts removed
½ pint light sweet cream
Salt and pepper to taste
2 tablespoons fresh dill, chopped
⅛ lb. butter
1 cup fine dry bread crumbs, prepared in blender and seasoned
3 tablespoons butter

With meat grinding attachment of mixer, grind together twice the chicken breasts, veal, and pork. Add eggs. Soak bread in cream, and when softened, pour mixture into meat, using all the cream even if not absorbed by the bread. Season and add dill. Cut the butter into tiny pieces and add to mixture. Mix thoroughly. Roll into rounded ovals, using an ice cream scoop for uniform measure. Do not flatten to fry. Roll in seasoned bread crumbs and fry in butter on griddle at 375° until golden but not brown, turning once. Cutlets should be pale. Remove to baking pan, cover with aluminum foil, and bake at 350° for 20 minutes. Cutlets will puff up and should be served immediately. Serves 10.

NOTE: To freeze, store cutlets when they have been browned, but not baked. Store in covered pan in freezer until ready to use. When needed, defrost and bake as above.

TURKEY WITH POTATO STUFFING*

1 8- to 10-lb. turkey
Turkey giblets
3 large potatoes, unpeeled
1 cup fine dry bread crumbs, prepared in blender
¼ lb. butter, melted
¼ cup hot milk
½ cup minced onion
½ teaspoon garlic salt
½ teaspoon salt
⅛ teaspoon pepper
1 egg, well beaten
Salt, pepper, garlic powder, and paprika to sprinkle inside and outside
   of bird
3 tablespoons salad oil

Boil turkey giblets and grind. Boil potatoes with jackets, and when soft, peel, cut into small pieces, and place in electric mixer bowl. Beat at slow speed, gradually adding melted butter alternately with hot milk. Beat until potatoes are fluffy. Add bread crumbs, seasonings, and beaten egg and blend. Add ground giblets. Cool.

Wash and dry turkey and season inside cavity. Fill with cooled stuffing. Fasten legs, rub skin with salad oil and season outside. Place bird breast-side-up on rack in roaster pan. Roast, uncovered, at 450° for about 20 minutes, then reduce heat to 325° and roast until tender, about 2½ hours. Baste frequently with drippings from pan. Serves 10 to 12.

HAM-CHEDDAR CHEESE PUFF*

2 cups milk
1 tablespoon butter
⅓ cup yellow cornmeal
1 cup sharp Cheddar cheese, shredded in blender
3 eggs, separated
¼ teaspoon salt
⅛ teaspoon paprika
1 cup cooked ham, ground in meat grinding attachment of mixer

Combine milk, butter, and cornmeal and cheese in saucepan. Bring to a boil and cook 5 minutes. Remove from heat and beat in egg yolks and seasoning. Add ham. Beat egg whites with electric beater until stiff; fold gently into ham mixture. Pour into greased 2-quart baking dish. Bake at 350° for 50 to 60 minutes or until tester inserted in the middle comes out clean. Serves 4.

SAUSAGE PUDDING*

8 pork sausages
½ cup sausage fat
2 eggs
1 cup cold milk
1 cup all-purpose flour
½ teaspoon salt

Fry sausages until completely cooked. Arrange sausages in a single layer in 8 x 8 x 2-inch pan. Add sausage fat. To prepare batter, beat eggs in electric mixer and add milk gradually, beating at slow speed. Add flour and salt, beating only until all flour lumps are moistened. Batter should be lumpy. Pour batter over sausage layer. Bake at 450° for 30 minutes. Puncture corners of pudding with fork to allow steam to escape. Turn off oven and allow pudding to dry for 10 minutes in oven. Serves 4 to 5.

RUSSIAN MEAT PIE*

MEAT FILLING

2 lbs. ground chuck
1 small onion, chopped
2 tablespoons butter
⅛ teaspoon garlic powder
2 tablespoons chopped fresh dill
½ teaspoon salt
⅛ teaspoon pepper
2 eggs, slightly beaten
3 hard-boiled eggs, chopped coarsely

Brown meat with onion in butter. Add seasonings and grind mixture with meat grinding attachment of electric mixer. Drain off excess liquid, stir in beaten eggs, and add chopped hard-boiled eggs. Fill pastry-lined baking pan, roll out other one-half of dough large enough to cover pie, and crimp edges. Pierce upper pastry with fork in several places. Bake at 350° for 1 hour, or until golden. Serves 12.

PASTRY

1 8-oz. package cream cheese, room temperature
½ lb. salted butter, room temperature
3 tablespoons vegetable shortening
3 tablespoons sour cream
2 cups all-purpose flour, sifted

With electric beater, combine cream cheese and butter; then add shortening and sour cream and blend well. Gradually beat in flour at medium speed, until thoroughly mixed. Form into ball, wrap in waxed paper, and chill until firm enough to handle easily. Roll one-half the dough on floured surface, about ¼ inch thick, to line bottom of ungreased 10½ x 15 x 2-inch baking pan.

NOTE: This may be frozen before or after baking, assembled or unassembled. If freezing meat mixture separately, omit hard-boiled eggs until ready to use for pie filling.

FISH CHEESE BAKE

2 lbs. haddock or halibut fillets
½ cup sour cream
½ cup sharp Cheddar cheese, grated in blender
2 eggs, separated
2 tablespoons chopped pimiento-stuffed olives
1 tablespoon finely chopped onion
½ teaspoon salt

Place washed and dried fish fillets in lightly greased, shallow 9 x 13 x 2-inch baking dish, arranging fillets in a single layer. Combine sour cream, cheese, egg yolks, olives, onion, and salt. With electric mixer, beat egg whites until stiff. Gently fold into sour cream mixture until well combined. Spread over fish, covering completely. Bake, uncovered, at 350° for 25 minutes or until fish flakes easily with fork and puff is golden. Serves 6.

Side Dishes

FILLED MASHED POTATO PATTIES*

6 large potatoes, pared and quartered
2 tablespoons salted butter
Salt and pepper to taste
2 eggs, beaten
3 tablespoons flour
1 cup chicken livers
1 large onion, cut up
3 tablespoons butter
Salt and pepper to taste
1 cup flour
⅛ lb. butter

Boil potatoes until soft. Mash with electric beaters while still hot, adding butter and seasoning. Gradually beat in eggs and flour and blend. Fry chicken livers and onion in butter until all red disappears and onions are limp. Season. Grind in meat grinding attachment of mixer. Form mashed potato mixture into small hamburger-sized patties. Make a dent in center of each patty, fill with 1 tablespoon of liver mixture, covering filled dent with more potato. Roll patties in flour and fry in butter until golden brown on both sides. Serves 6 to 8.

POTATO-CARROT CAKES*

4 cups seasoned mashed potatoes, prepared in mixer as above
4 large whole cooked carrots
1 cup cracker meal
1 teaspoon salt
2 teaspoons butter or bacon fat

Wrap 1 cup of mashed potatoes around each carrot. Roll up in waxed paper and chill. When ready to serve, slice each roll into 5 to 6 cakes and dip in cracker meal and salt. Pan fry in butter or bacon fat until golden. Serves 5 to 6.

FILLED BAKED POTATOES*

3 large hot baked potatoes
¾ teaspoon seasoned salt
½ teaspoon salt
¼ teaspoon pepper
¼ cup diced green pepper
1 tablespoon minced onion
1 tablespoon salad oil
¼ cup diced fresh tomato
¼ cup finely chopped ham
Fresh parsley for garnish

Split baked potatoes in half lengthwise and scoop out the centers, leaving shells intact. Mash with electric beaters until fluffy and add seasonings. Sauté green pepper and onion in salad oil, add tomato, and cook until glossy but not limp. Stir into the potato mixture and add ham. Put back into potato shells and bake at 375° for 10 to 15 minutes or until browned. Garnish with parsley. Serves 6.

SWEET POTATO PUDDING*

2 tablespoons brown sugar
1 teaspoon cinnamon
2 cups canned applesauce
1 tablespoon grated orange rind
3 cups sweet potatoes, cooked or canned and mashed in mixer
¾ teaspoon salt
⅓ cup melted butter
4 eggs, separated

Combine sugar and cinnamon. Add to applesauce with orange rind and mix well. Combine mashed sweet potatoes with applesauce mixture, salt, and melted butter. Add beaten egg yolks. With electric beater, whip egg whites until stiff. Gently fold into potato mixture. Pile lightly into greased 3-quart casserole. Bake at 400° for 45 minutes. Serves 6 to 8.

SWEET POTATO-PINEAPPLE BAKE*

4 cups sweet potatoes, cooked or canned and mashed in mixer
½ cup hot milk
⅛ lb. sweet butter, melted
¼ cup brown sugar
¼ cup honey
¾ cup crushed pineapple, drained
Cinnamon and nutmeg to taste
1 cup miniature marshmallows

Whip mashed sweet potatoes in mixer with milk and butter. Beat in brown sugar and honey, adjusting sweetness to taste. Stir in crushed pineapple. Season with cinnamon and nutmeg. Place in 2-quart casserole, top with layer of miniature marshmallows, and bake at 350° for 30 to 35 minutes, or until marshmallows are melted and golden brown. Serves 8.

SWEET POTATO MERINGUE*

2 cups sweet potatoes, mashed in electric mixer
½ cup brown sugar
½ teaspoon salt
¼ cup orange juice
1 teaspoon grated orange rind
2 tablespoons butter
½ cup light cream
3 eggs, separated
3 tablespoons granulated sugar

Combine mashed potatoes with all ingredients except egg whites and granulated sugar. Pour into greased 2-quart casserole and bake at 325° for 30 minutes. Beat egg whites in mixer until foamy, add granulated sugar and beat until stiff. Spread meringue on top of baked sweet potato mixture and return to oven, baking at 400° for 3 to 4 minutes, or until meringue is golden brown. Serves 4 to 6.

SWEET POTATO, APPLE, AND ORANGE LAYERS*

1 cup sugar
4 tablespoons cornstarch
¾ teaspoon salt
¼ teaspoon nutmeg
½ cup orange juice
1½ cups water
1 teaspoon grated orange rind
¼ lb. butter
7 sweet potatoes, boiled, peeled, and sliced
7 apples, pared, cored, and sliced

Mix sugar, cornstarch, salt, and nutmeg together in saucepan. Add orange juice and water gradually, beating with electric beaters to blend thoroughly. Heat, continuing to beat slowly until mixture comes to a boil. Remove from heat and add grated orange rind and butter, stirring until butter is melted. Arrange potatoes and apples in alternating layers in 8 to 12-inch shallow baking dish, having potatoes as bottom and top layers. Pour sauce over the layers and bake at 350° for 1 hour, or until apples are tender. Serves 8.

CABBAGE PATTIES*

1 head green cabbage (about 3 lbs.)
3 tablespoons butter
3 tablespoons flour
1 cup milk
3 eggs, beaten
1½ cups dry bread crumbs
1 tablespoon salt
1 teaspoon pepper
1 teaspoon caraway seeds

Core and chop cabbage. Rinse cabbage under cold water and then simmer in boiling water for about 6 minutes. Drain, cool slightly, and put through meat grinding attachment of mixer. Drain again. Place butter in saucepan and heat gently. When butter is melted, blend in flour with electric beater at slow speed. Continue heating and add milk, all at once, beating to blend thoroughly. Add sauce, beaten eggs, bread crumbs, salt, pepper, and caraway seeds to cabbage. Mix well and spread in large shallow pan. Chill 1 hour. Shape in flat patties, roll in flour, and brown on both sides in hot fat. Makes about 18 patties.

EGGPLANT-ZUCCHINI SOUFFLÉ

1 large eggplant, peeled and cubed
2 medium-sized zucchini, peeled and cubed
3 tablespoons butter
3 tablespoons flour
1 cup milk
½ cup grated Parmesan cheese
¾ cup seasoned dry bread crumbs
¼ cup finely chopped onion
2 tablespoons tomato sauce
Dash of cayenne pepper
Salt and pepper to taste
3 eggs, separated

Place eggplant and zucchini in salted boiling water and simmer until tender. Drain and mash with electric beaters. Prepare white sauce by placing butter in saucepan. Heat gently, and when melted, blend in flour with electric beaters, at slow speed. Continue beating and add milk all at once, beating to blend thoroughly. Remove from heat and stir in cheese and bread crumbs. Add onion, tomato sauce, and seasoning. Add egg yolks and return to heat. Bring to a boil and remove from heat. With electric beater, beat egg whites until stiff; fold them into mixture. Pour into a buttered 1½-quart soufflé dish; set in pan of hot water. Set on top of stove and bring water in pan to a boil. Place in oven and bake 30 to 40 minutes, or until soufflé appears dry in center and is lightly browned. Serves 6.

SPINACH SOUFFLÉ

1 10-oz. package frozen, chopped spinach, cooked according to package instructions and drained
5 eggs, separated
4 tablespoons flour
4 tablespoons butter, softened
¾ cup hot milk
1 teaspoon salt
⅛ teaspoon pepper

Combine spinach, egg yolks, flour, butter, milk, and seasoning in saucepan and cook over low heat, stirring until thick. Remove from heat and cool. In electric mixer, beat egg whites until stiff, and fold in spinach mixture. Bake in 1½-quart casserole at 375° for 30 minutes. Serves 4.

POPOVERS*

2 eggs
1 tablespoon shortening
⅞ cup milk
1 cup all-purpose flour, sifted
1 teaspoon salt

Cream eggs with shortening in electric mixer. Add milk and flour alternately, beating well. Add salt and blend well. Use greased 2½-inch Pyrex cups, filled half full. Bake at 425° for 45 minutes. Serve to accompany dinner. Makes 10.

Desserts

RUM WHIP

3 egg yolks
½ cup sugar
¼ cup light rum
1 tablespoon gelatin
¼ cup cold water
1 pint heavy cream

In electric mixer, beat the egg yolks at medium speed until lemon colored. Add sugar gradually and beat until very light and thick. Add rum. Soften gelatin in cold water and heat this mixture over boiling water until dissolved. Add to egg mixture and beat several minutes. Chill until mixture begins to set. Whip heavy cream and fold into egg mixture. Turn into 1½-quart mold and chill until firm. Serves 8.

NOTE: To use leftover egg whites, which may be frozen until ready to use, see recipe for coconut meringues on p. 187.

COCONUT MERINGUES

3 egg whites
¼ teaspoon salt
½ teaspoon vanilla
1 cup confectioners' sugar, sifted
1 6-oz. package semisweet chocolate bits
1 cup flaked coconut
2 cups corn flakes

In electric mixer, combine egg whites, salt, and vanilla and beat at high speed until stiff, but not dry. Beat in sugar gradually, until stiff. Fold in remaining ingredients. Drop by teaspoonfuls on well-greased cookie sheet. Bake at 350° for 18 to 20 minutes. Yields 3½ dozen cookies.

BAKED PLUM PUDDING*

¼ cup butter
½ cup light brown sugar
1½ cups all-purpose flour, sifted
1¼ teaspoons double-acting baking powder
¼ teaspoon salt
⅓ cup butter
½ cup granulated sugar
1 teaspoon grated orange rind
1 egg
½ cup orange juice
2 lbs. Italian plums, pitted and cut in half, sugared lightly

Melt butter in 8 x 8 x 2-inch baking pan. Remove from heat. Mix in brown sugar and spread evenly over bottom of pan. Sift together flour, baking powder, and salt. In electric mixer, slowly cream butter, granulated sugar, and orange rind. Beat in egg.

Beat in sifted ingredients, alternating with orange juice, until smooth. Place mixture in baking pan and cover with sugared, halved plums, skin side up. Bake at 350° for 40 to 45 minutes or until cake tester inserted in center comes out clean. Cool and cut. Serves 8.

APPLE DESSERT*

4 cups apples, peeled, cored, and sliced
½ cup sugar
½ teaspoon cinnamon
¾ cup walnut meats, coarsely broken
1 cup all-purpose flour, sifted
¼ teaspoon salt
1 teaspoon baking powder
1 egg
½ cup evaporated milk
⅓ cup butter, melted
¼ cup nut meats to decorate top

Spread apples on bottom of greased 9 x 13 x 2-inch baking pan. Sprinkle with mixture of sugar, cinnamon, and walnuts. Sift together flour, salt, and baking powder. In electric mixer, combine egg, milk, and melted butter. Gradually beat in dry ingredients at slow speed. Pour batter over apples and sprinkle nuts on top. Bake at 350° for 50 minutes. Serves 12.

WALNUT CRESCENTS*

½ **cup butter**
½ **cup vegetable shortening**
⅓ **cup sugar**
2 **cups all-purpose flour, sifted**
2 **teaspoons water**
2 **teaspoons vanilla**
½ **cup walnuts, ground in blender**

Cream butter and shortening with sugar in electric mixer at medium speed. Add flour, water, and vanilla. Blend well, then add nuts. Batter will be very stiff and will need to be removed from beaters manually. Refrigerate for at least an hour. Shape into balls 1 inch in diameter, roll into oblong strips, and form into crescents. Place on ungreased cookie sheet and bake at 350° for 20 minutes, or until lightly golden. Makes 8 dozen.

PECAN SQUARES*

½ **cup butter**
1 **cup sugar**
1 **egg, separated**
2 **cups all-purpose flour, sifted**
1 **teaspoon vanilla**
¼ **cup pecans, chopped briefly in blender**

In electric mixer, cream together at medium speed butter and sugar until light. Add egg yolk and blend well. Add flour and vanilla. Press half the dough into bottom of ungreased 10 x 15 x ¼-inch jelly-roll pan. Mixture will be thick. Sprinkle with half the pecans, then cover with remaining dough. Beat egg white, spread over sheet, and sprinkle with balance of nuts. Bake at 350° for 20 minutes. Cut into 2-inch squares. Makes about 3 dozen.

ORANGE NUT CAKE*

2 cups sugar
¾ cup shortening
3 eggs
3 cups all-purpose flour, sifted
1½ teaspoons baking soda
1 teaspoon salt
1 cup milk
1 cup raisins
1 cup walnuts, chopped coarsely in blender
1 teaspoon vanilla
1 cup orange juice
¼ cup sugar
1 teaspoon grated orange rind

In electric mixer, cream together sugar and shortening until light and fluffy. Add eggs. Sift together flour, soda, and salt, and add to slowly beating mixer alternately with milk. When well blended, add raisins, nuts, and vanilla. Bake in greased and floured 9-inch tube pan at 350° for 1 hour. Remove from pan and, while cake is still warm, pour on orange juice which has been combined with sugar and grated orange rind. Serves 10.

CHOCOLATE DATE CAKE*

½ cup butter
½ cup vegetable shortening
¾ cup sugar
2 eggs
1 7-oz. package pitted dates
1 teaspoon baking soda
1 cup boiling water
1¾ cups flour, sifted
2 heaping tablespoons cocoa
½ teaspoon salt
1 teaspoon vanilla
1 3-oz. package semisweet chocolate chips
½ cup walnut meats, chopped coarsely in blender

In electric mixer, cream butter and shortening with sugar at medium speed until light and fluffy. Add eggs and blend. Cut dates into small pieces into bowl, and add baking soda and boiling water. Mix flour, cocoa, and salt and fold into batter, alternating with date mixture. Add vanilla and one-half the chocolate chips. Mix together and pour into 9 x 13 x 2-inch baking pan. Spread remaining chocolate chips and nuts over top of batter. Bake at 350° for 40 minutes. Serves 12.

DATE AND NUT TORTE*

2 eggs, separated
1 cup brown sugar, firmly packed
½ cup flour, sifted
½ teaspoon baking powder
½ teaspoon salt
½ cup walnut meats, chopped coarsely in blender
1 cup pitted dates, cut up
½ pint heavy sweet cream

In electric mixer, beat egg yolks with brown sugar at medium speed. Sift together flour, baking powder, and salt; add nut meats and dates, tossing to coat evenly. Stir into egg yolk mixture. Beat egg whites until stiff and fold gently into egg and flour mixture. Pour into greased 8 x 8 x 2-inch baking pan and bake at 325° for 35 minutes, or until cake tester inserted in the middle comes out clean. Cut into pieces and serve topped with whipped cream. Serves 6.

BUTTERSCOTCH CHEWY CAKE*

1½ cups flour, sifted
1½ teaspoons baking powder
4 eggs
2 cups dark brown sugar, firmly packed
1 tablespoon butter
1½ cups nuts, chopped in blender
1 teaspoon vanilla
Ice cream for topping

Sift together flour and baking powder. Place eggs in top of double boiler and beat with electric beater until just blended. Add brown sugar and butter and beat until butter is melted, and mixture is just hot. Remove from heat. Add flour mixture all at once. Beat until well blended. Stir in nuts and vanilla. Bake in greased and floured 9 x 13 x 2-inch pan at 350° for 25 to 30 minutes. Cut in pan. Serves 10 to 12.

CHOCOLATE COCONUT CAKE*

½ cup butter
3 squares unsweetened baking chocolate, melted
1 cup buttermilk
1 teaspoon vanilla
1¾ cups cake flour, sifted
1½ cups sugar
¾ teaspoon salt
½ teaspoon baking powder
¾ teaspoon baking soda
2 eggs
1 cup coconut
½ cup walnut meats, broken into small pieces

In electric mixer, cream butter, add melted chocolate, buttermilk, and vanilla at slow speed, and beat well. Sift together cake flour, sugar, salt, baking powder, and baking soda, and add to first mixture. Add eggs and beat well. Fold in coconut and walnuts. Place in greased 9-inch layer pans which have been lined with waxed paper. Bake at 375° for 30 minutes, or until cake tester inserted in center comes out clean. Cool, turn out, and ice between layers and on top and sides. Serves 10 to 12.

DARK FUDGE ICING

4 squares unsweetened baking chocolate
1¼ cups boiling water
3 tablespoons butter
1½ cups sugar
3 tablespoons cornstarch
1 teaspoon vanilla

Melt chocolate in boiling water, add butter and sugar, and stir over heat until melted. Make paste of cornstarch and some of the chocolate mixture, then stir in and cook until icing thickens. Add vanilla. Cool slightly before spreading.

DOUBLE CHOCOLATE LAYER CAKE*

1¾ cups all-purpose flour, sifted
1½ cups sugar
1¼ teaspoons double-acting baking powder
½ teaspoon baking soda
1 teaspoon salt
½ cup vegetable shortening
1 cup milk
1 teaspoon vanilla
2 eggs
2 squares unsweetened baking chocolate, melted
½ teaspoon red food coloring

Sift together into mixer bowl, flour, sugar, baking powder, baking soda, and salt. Add shortening, milk, and vanilla, beating at medium speed until well blended, about 2 minutes. Add eggs, melted chocolate, and food coloring, and beat for another 2 minutes at medium speed. Pour into well-greased and floured 8-inch layer pans and bake at 375° for 30 to 35 minutes, or until cake tester inserted in center comes out clean. When cool, turn out layers and ice. Serves 8 to 10.

MEDIUM CHOCOLATE ICING

1 egg
2 cups confectioners' sugar, sifted
¼ teaspoon salt
⅓ cup vegetable shortening, soft
2 squares unsweetened baking chocolate, melted
1 teaspoon vanilla

Beat together with electric mixer all above ingredients until smooth.

QUICK POUND CAKE*

1 cup vegetable shortening
2 cups sugar
4 eggs
3 cups all-purpose flour, sifted
4 teaspoons baking powder
1 cup milk
1 teaspoon lemon extract
1 teaspoon vanilla extract

In electric mixer, cream together shortening and sugar, add eggs, and beat at medium speed until well mixed. Sift together flour and baking powder and add alternately with milk, continuing to beat until well blended. Add extracts. Bake in 8-inch greased and floured tube pan at 350° for 1 hour, or until golden and cake tester comes out dry. Serve plain or with ice cream. Serves 10 to 12.

FRENCH COFFEE CAKE*

½ cup butter
½ cup vegetable shortening
1½ cups sugar
5 eggs
1 cup sour cream
3 cups all-purpose flour, sifted
2 teaspoons baking powder
1 teaspoon baking soda
1 teaspoon vanilla

TOPPING

1 teaspoon cinnamon
½ cup sugar
1 cup broken walnut meats
2 squares baking chocolate, grated in blender

Cream butter and shortening with sugar. Add eggs and sour cream and mix well. Sift flour with baking powder and baking soda and beat in gradually. When well mixed, stir in vanilla. Combine topping ingredients. Place half the batter in greased and floured 10-inch tube pan. Sprinkle with half the topping, using knife to cut it in. Cover with remaining batter, and repeat with rest of topping. Bake at 350° for 45 minutes or until cake tester inserted in middle comes out clean. Serves 10 to 12.

ORANGE MERINGUE PIE

1 baked 9-inch pie shell (see p. 89)
¾ cup sugar
¼ cup cornstarch
⅛ teaspoon salt
1 cup orange juice
½ cup water
1 tablespoon lemon juice
3 eggs, separated
1 tablespoon grated orange rind
1 tablespoon butter
⅛ teaspoon salt
6 tablespoons sugar

Combine ¾ cup sugar, cornstarch, and salt in a medium saucepan. Slowly blend in orange juice, water, and lemon juice. Cook and stir over medium heat until mixture is thickened and clear. Beat egg yolks lightly in electric mixer bowl. At very slow speed, gradually beat in hot mixture, until just blended. Add orange rind and butter and cool thoroughly. Spoon into baked pie shell. With mixer, beat egg whites with salt until frothy. Add sugar gradually, beating well after each addition. Continue to beat until stiff peaks are formed. With spoon, place mounds of meringue over filling and spread to cover completely. Bake at 350° for 12 to 15 minutes, or until meringue is golden. Chill. Serves 8 to 10.

Five

The Electric Frying Pan

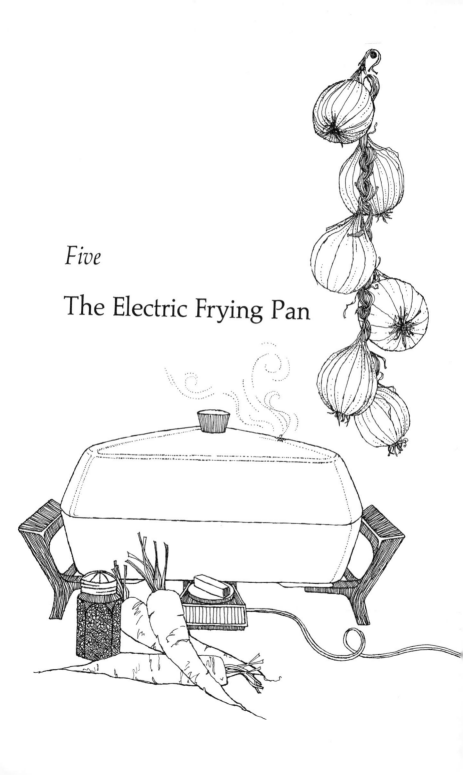

The Electric Frying Pan

IF YOU DON'T OWN an electric frying pan or if you don't often use the one you own, you're missing many opportunities for simple meal preparation. The electric frying pan is not only easy to use, it is so versatile that it can be at your service for breakfast, lunch, dinner, and quick, hot snacks. Because it maintains constant, exact heat, the electric frying pan is ideal for all sorts of foods that usually need close watching. Blueberry pancakes, Fried Chicken in Cream Sauce, and even Sukiyaki turn out perfectly every time.

You'll naturally want to use your frying pan for eggs, French toast, and other breakfast favorites. And try it for grilled sandwiches for lunch. It can also double as a chafing dish from which you can serve delectable hot appetizers. Next time you're having guests serve them Sweet and Sour Cocktail Meatballs, Shrimp in Soy-Sherry Sauce, or Sausage and Pineapple Kebabs. Perhaps the best use of all for the electric frying pan is in braising meats and poultry—you can brown and braise in the same pan at just the right temperature.

The new cook will find the electric frying pan to be the ideal appliance. By using it, the beginner can tackle a wide variety of dishes with perfect assurance. In fact, I know one young woman who for the first six months of her marriage prepared delicious meals using only an electric frying pan and a hot plate. She often asked me for recipes and one of her favorites was sautéed chicken breasts in wine sauce, which became famous among her friends. She even used her frying pan to bake meat loaf, cakes, garlic bread, and foil-wrapped potatoes.

I hope the recipes in this section will show you how to turn your electric frying pan into one of your greatest allies in the kitchen.

Appetizers

SAUSAGE AND PINEAPPLE KEBABS*

1 lb. sweet Italian sausage
1 16-oz. can pineapple chunks, drained

In electric skillet, at 325°, fry sausage links until well browned on both sides and thoroughly cooked through. Cut into 1-inch pieces and combine with pineapple chunks, heating until chunks are hot and lightly browned. Using wooden toothpicks, skewer sausage and a pineapple chunk on each toothpick and serve hot. Serves 12 to 14.

COCKTAIL MEATBALLS PICCALILLI*

2 tablespoons butter
1 lb. ground beef
1 egg
1 slice white bread, with crust removed
3 tablespoons milk
Salt and pepper to taste
1 10-oz. jar sweet pickle relish

Melt butter in electric frypan. In a bowl, mix together meat, egg, and bread which has been softened in milk and seasonings. Shape into 1-inch meatballs and fry at 325° until evenly brown on all sides. When done, pour in sweet pickle relish and heat through, stirring to distribute evenly. Serve hot. Serves 10 to 12.

MUSHROOMS IN TART SHELLS

4 tablespoons butter
1 clove garlic, minced
1 lb. mushrooms, sliced
2 tablespoons chopped dill
Salt and pepper to taste
1 cup sour cream

Melt butter in electric frypan, add garlic, and brown slightly. Add mushrooms, dill, and seasonings. Cook at 325° until mushrooms are soft. Turn off heat, and stir in sour cream. Spoon mushrooms into tiny appetizer tart shells, which may be bought ready made, (or make your own pastry, using one-half the recipe for hot pastry canapés, see p. 12). Serve hot. Serves 8.

SHRIMP IN SHERRY

2 lbs. raw shrimp
3 tablespoons soy sauce
1 tablespoon fresh ginger, chopped
1 cup cooking sherry

Shell and devein shrimp. In electric skillet, combine soy sauce, ginger, and sherry, and heat until liquid begins to bubble. Add shrimp, cover with fry pan lid, closing air vent so that no steam will escape. Turn temperature control to 300° and allow to simmer 25 minutes, turning shrimp at least once. Serve drained and hot with toothpicks. Serves 8.

SWEET-AND-SOUR MEATBALLS*

2 lbs. ground round
2 medium onions, each chopped separately in blender
1 egg
1 teaspoon salt
1 teaspoon paprika
½ cup cold water
½ cup dry bread crumbs
2 tablespoons butter
½ cup seedless raisins
½ cup boiling water
5 gingersnaps, finely crumbled in blender
½ cup brown sugar
¼ cup cider vinegar

Combine beef, 1 chopped onion, egg, salt, and paprika. Add cold water and bread crumbs and work well to mix thoroughly. With wet hands, shape into ¾-inch meatballs. Brown other chopped onion in butter in electric frypan at 350°, add meatballs, and brown on all sides, shaking pan to keep balls round. When done, add pickled beet, raisins, and boiling water. Cover frypan and simmer at 225° for 45 minutes. Then add gingersnap crumbs and brown sugar, and cook for 20 minutes more. Serve hot. Serves 12 to 14.

NOTE: These meatballs taste best when made a day before and reheated before serving.

FRIED DEVILED EGGS

6 eggs, hard-boiled and cooled in shell
2 tablespoons mayonnaise
1 tablespoon prepared mustard
Salt and pepper to taste
2 tablespoons seasoned bread crumbs
3 tablespoons butter
Chopped dill or parsley

With very sharp knife, using quick, sharp movements, cut unpeeled hard-boiled eggs lengthwise, and remove whites and yolks from shells. Chop fine and mix with mayonnaise, mustard, and seasonings. Fill shells flat, sprinkling with seasoned bread crumbs. Melt butter in electric skillet and place egg shells face down, frying until heated through at 325°. Remove from frypan with spatula, decorate with chopped dill or chopped parsley, and serve hot. Serves 6.

Main Dishes

FRIED CHICKEN IN CREAM SAUCE*

2½ lb. frying chicken, cut up
½ cup flour
1½ teaspoons salt
¾ teaspoon pepper
4 tablespoons butter
4 tablespoons vegetable shortening
2 tablespoons flour
2 cups light cream

Shake chicken pieces in paper bag with flour, salt, and pepper. In electric frypan, at 375° melt butter and shortening, add chicken, and brown quickly on all sides. Reduce heat to 325°, cover, and continue frying for 25 minutes, turning occasionally. Remove cover during last 10 minutes of cooking. When chicken is done, remove from skillet and drain off all but 2 tablespoons of fat. Stir in flour and add cream gradually, stirring constantly. Adjust seasoning, if desired, and cook until thickened. Pour over chicken. Serves 4.

CURRIED CHICKEN BREASTS WITH APPLE

3 whole chicken breasts, split and boned
¼ lb. butter
1 large onion, chopped in blender
1 peeled apple, chopped coarsely in blender
¾ cup light cream
1 tablespoon curry powder

In electric frying pan, sauté chicken breasts in butter at 375°. Turn frequently so that they do not turn too brown. Remove. Cook onion and apple in same butter until limp, but not brown. Add ½ cup of light cream, reserving the other ¼ cup. Dissolve curry powder in remaining light cream, then add to onion and apple mixture. Return breasts to skillet, cover, and let simmer at 250° until tender. If sauce thickens, add more cream immediately before serving to restore smoothness. Serves 6.

CHICKEN BREASTS SAUTERNE*

3 tablespoons olive oil
2 tablespoons butter
3 whole chicken breasts, split and boned
Salt and pepper to taste
1 lb. fresh mushrooms, sliced
3 tablespoons flour
1 cup sauterne
½ cup water

In electric frying pan, combine oil and butter and heat at 360°. Season chicken breasts and add; turning often, cook until delicately brown and tender, about 20 minutes. Add mushrooms and continue cooking until they are tender, about 15 minutes. Cover pan and steam for 15 minutes at 250°. Remove chicken breasts and mushrooms to heated platter and keep warm. Reheat frying pan to 360°, add flour and brown, stirring constantly. Add wine all at once, stirring constantly and allowing to evaporate. Stir in water to make sauce. Pour sauce over breasts. Serves 6.

CHICKEN LIVERS SAUTÉ*

1 strip bacon
1 small onion, diced
1 lb. chicken livers
2 tablespoons all-purpose flour
1 cup clear canned chicken broth
1 lb. fresh mushrooms
½ teaspoon lemon juice
Salt and pepper to taste

Render bacon in electric skillet at 400°. Add onion and sauté until browned. Toss chicken livers in flour, and add to bacon and onion in frypan. Sauté at 350° for 7 to 8 minutes. Add chicken broth, mushrooms, lemon juice, and salt and pepper, stirring to make smooth gravy. Serves 4.

DRUMSTICKS WITH CRANBERRY TOPPING*

6 chicken legs with thighs
½ cup all-purpose flour
1 teaspoon salt
¼ teaspoon pepper
⅓ cup vegetable shortening

CRANBERRY TOPPING

½ **lb. fresh cranberries**
¾ **cup sugar**
1 **cup water**
¼ **cup lemon juice**
¼ **cup prepared horseradish**

Boil sugar and water together until bubbly. Add cranberries and boil without stirring until all berries pop open, about 6 minutes. Cool in pan. Stir in lemon juice and horseradish.

Dredge drumsticks in flour, which has been seasoned with salt and pepper. In electric skillet, melt shortening and brown at 325°, cooking about 30 minutes, turning occasionally. Spoon half the topping over browned drumsticks. Cover and simmer at 275° for another 25 minutes, or until tender. Spoon on remaining topping and cook 10 minutes longer. Serves 4 to 6.

BEEF-PRUNE STEW*

2½ **lbs. boneless chuck, in 1½-inch cubes**
¼ **cup flour**
2 **teaspoons salt**
¼ **teaspoon pepper**
¼ **teaspoon paprika**
3 **tablespoons salad oil**
6 **potatoes, quartered**
1 **lb. dry prunes, soaked in water for 2 hours and pitted**
2 **large onions, chopped in blender**
2 **carrots, cut in 2-inch pieces**
2 **tablespoons brown sugar**
Juice of 1 lemon

Dredge meat in flour mixed with the salt, pepper, and paprika. In electric skillet, at 400°, heat oil and brown meat on all sides. Add the water in which the prunes were soaked. Cover and simmer at 225° for 1½ hours. Add prunes and cook for ½ hour or until meat is almost tender. Add onions, carrots, potatoes, lemon juice, and sugar, and continue cooking until vegetables are tender, about 35 minutes more. Serves 6.

SUKIYAKI

1½ lbs. beef sirloin tips, sliced across the grain into ¼-inch strips
3 tablespoons vegetable oil
½ lb. fresh mushrooms, sliced
1 green pepper, cut in squares
1 large onion, sliced
3 ribs celery, bias-cut into slices
3 scallions, sliced
1 4-oz. can bamboo shoots, drained and diced
1 4-oz. can water chestnuts, drained and sliced
3 tablespoons water
⅓ cup soy sauce
1 beef bouillon cube, dissolved in ½ cup hot water
2 cups hot cooked rice

In electric skillet, at 400°, brown meat in oil. Add all ingredients except rice and cover, lowering heat to 275°. Cook about 10 minutes, or until meat is tender but vegetables are still crisp and retain their color. Stir gently so that ingredients retain original shapes. Serve with hot rice. Serves 4 to 6.

BARBECUED BEEF FLANK STEAK*

1½ lbs. flank steak
2 tablespoons flour
½ teaspoon salt
Dash pepper
2 tablespoons shortening
1 clove garlic, minced
1 medium onion, sliced
1 10½-oz. can beef gravy
¼ cup chili sauce
½ teaspoon dry mustard
1 tablespoon chopped parsley

Score both sides of steak by making shallow diagonal cuts about ¾ inch apart. With meat hammer, pound in flour seasoned with salt and pepper. In electric frypan, brown steak in shortening on both sides at 400°. Add garlic and onion. Combine gravy, chili sauce, and mustard and pour over meat. Cover. Cook at 220° for 2 hours, spooning sauce over steak periodically. Sprinkle with chopped parsley. Serves 6.

HAMBURGERS IN CAPER SAUCE

2 lbs. ground chuck
½ cup evaporated milk
1 egg, slightly beaten
1 teaspoon salt
¼ teaspoon pepper
¼ teaspoon monosodium glutamate
¼ teaspoon garlic powder

Mix meat, evaporated milk, eggs, and seasonings. Shape meat into 8 patties and pan broil in electric skillet at 350°, turning once and cooking for about 10 minutes on each side, or according to your preference. Remove to warm platter. Prepare sauce.

CAPER SAUCE

3 tablespoons butter
3 tablespoons sour cream
4 tablespoons capers

Place butter in unwashed frying pan, add sour cream and capers, and heat through, stirring well. Pour over meat. Serves 4 to 5.

QUICK MEAT LOAF

1½ lbs. ground chuck
½ green pepper, chopped in blender
½ medium onion, chopped in blender
1 rib celery, chopped in blender
1 cup corn flakes
1 egg, beaten slightly
1 teaspoon salt
¼ teaspoon Worcestershire sauce
1 tablespoon ketchup
¼ teaspoon prepared mustard
1 tablespoon butter

Combine all ingredients except butter. Melt butter in electric frying pan and set at 375°. Add meat mixture and press down with spatula to conform to shape of pan. Brown 10 minutes. Cover and cook at 275° for about 20 minutes. Turn out on hot platter and prepare sauce (see p. 212).

MUSHROOM SAUCE

½ medium onion, chopped in blender
½ lb. fresh mushrooms, sliced
3 tablespoons butter
Salt and pepper to taste
¼ cup sour cream

Place chopped onion, mushrooms, and butter in unwashed frying pan and sauté at 300° until soft. Turn off heat, stir in sour cream, and pour over meat loaf. Serves 4.

VEAL SAUTÉ*

2½ lbs. boneless veal, cut in 1½-inch cubes
Salt and pepper to taste
2 tablespoons butter
2 tablespoons vegetable oil
5 medium onions, chopped in blender
¼ cup all-purpose flour
6 large tomatoes, peeled and quartered
1 cup sauterne
1 cup beef bouillon
1 clove garlic, minced
1 cup fresh mushrooms, sliced
¾ lb. egg noodles, cooked and buttered

Season meat. Combine butter and oil in electric skillet and heat to 375°. Brown meat and onions, then stir in flour, tomatoes, wine, and bouillon. Add garlic. Cover, lower heat to 250°, and simmer for about 1½ hours. Add mushrooms and continue to simmer, covered, for another 15 minutes or until meat is tender. Serve with buttered noodles. Serves 6.

VEAL IN CREAM SAUCE

1½ lbs. veal scallops
¼ cup flour
Salt and pepper to taste
3 tablespoons butter
3 tablespoons salad oil
1 medium onion, sliced and separated into rings
1 green pepper, cut in rings
½ cup sauterne
1 10-oz. can cream of chicken soup, undiluted
⅛ teaspoon ginger

Dust veal scallops with flour which has been seasoned with salt and pepper. In electric skillet, at 400°, mix together butter and oil, add meat and brown quickly on both sides. Remove from pan. Sauté onion and pepper rings lightly; add wine and soup. Return meat to pan, cover, and simmer at 275° for 15 to 20 minutes, or until meat is tender. Serves 4.

PORK CHOPS IN ORANGE SAUCE*

4 pork chops, about 1 inch thick
3 tablespoons all-purpose flour
Salt and pepper to taste
1 tablespoon vegetable shortening
2 large oranges, peeled and sectioned
2 tablespoons brown sugar
1 tablespoon cornstarch
⅛ teaspoon ground allspice
1¼ cups chicken broth
Juice of 1 lemon
Juice of 1 orange
¼ cup seedless golden raisins

Dredge chops in flour, salt, and pepper. Brown on both sides in electric skillet in shortening at 375°. Place orange sections on chops. Mix sugar, cornstarch, and allspice, and sprinkle over meat. Add broth and stir until thickened. Add juices and raisins, cover, and simmer at 225° for 40 minutes, or until tender. Serves 4.

LAMB CURRY

1½ lbs. lamb, boned and cut in 1-inch cubes
½ cup chopped onion
3 tablespoons butter
1½ cups hot water
1½ teaspoons curry powder
1 bay leaf, crushed
1½ teaspoons salt
¼ teaspoon pepper
2 tablespoons flour
¼ cup water
½ cup peeled, cubed apple
½ cup seedless raisins
2 tablespoons orange marmalade
¼ cup heavy sweet cream at room temperature
2 cups hot cooked rice

In electric skillet, at 400°, brown lamb and onions in butter. Stir in water, curry powder, bay leaf, salt, and pepper. Cover and simmer at 225°, adding a little more water if necessary, 30 minutes, or until meat is tender. Stir occasionally. Combine flour and ¼ cup water into smooth paste; stir into pan until slightly thickened. Stir in apple, raisins, and marmalade. Turn off heat, cool slightly, stir in cream and serve immediately over hot rice. Serves 4.

SAUSAGE CREOLE*

1 lb. pork sausage links
2 cups tomato sauce
Salt and pepper to taste
½ cup pineapple juice
½ cup chopped onion
½ cup chopped green pepper
1 tablespoon brown sugar
1 teaspoon Worcestershire sauce
2 to 3 cups hot cooked rice

In electric skillet, at 350°, cook sausage until brown and thoroughly cooked. Rmove sausage and discard drippings. Add remaining ingredients, except rice, and simmer, uncovered, at 280°, for 25 minutes, or until thickened. Add sausage links, heat, and serve on hot rice. Serves 4 to 5.

EGYPTIAN EGGPLANT*

1 large eggplant, peeled and sliced thin
1 tablespoon salt
¼ cup salad oil
2 large onions, chopped in blender
3 tablespoons butter
1 lb. ground round
1 6-oz. can tomato paste
1 cup hot water
Salt, pepper, and garlic powder to taste

Sprinkle eggplant with salt and let stand in water for 30 minutes. Rinse and dry. Sauté eggplant in oil at 375° until soft. Remove from pan. Sauté onions in butter, add meat, tomato paste, hot water, and seasonings and simmer 15 minutes at 325°. Place alternate layers of eggplant and meat mixture in casserole and bake at 350° for 1 hour. Serves 6.

GARLIC CLAMS

2 cloves garlic, minced
¼ cup salad oil
24 hard-shelled clams, thoroughly scrubbed and rinsed
Salt and pepper to taste
3 tablespoons tomato juice
Juice of 1 lemon
4 sprigs parsley, chopped
1 lemon, cut in wedges

In electric skillet, at 375°, sauté garlic in salad oil. When hot, add clams in their shells and salt, pepper, and tomato juice. Cover, closing air vent. Steam at 300° until clams open. Add lemon juice and chopped parsley, shake pan to distribute, and heat a few more minutes. Serve hot with lemon wedges. Serves 4.

FISH FILLETS WITH GREEN GRAPES

3 tablespoons butter
1½ lbs. fresh fish fillets (any fish is acceptable)
Salt and pepper to taste
1 clove garlic, minced
1 medium onion, minced
2 scallions, cut fine
¼ cup water
Juice of 1 lemon
2 teaspoons flour
¼ cup light sweet cream
2 cups fresh seedless green grapes, peeled

In electric skillet at 360°, melt 2 tablespoons butter and add fish fillets. Season with salt and pepper. Add minced garlic. Cover fillets with onions and scallions, and add water and lemon juice. Raise heat to 400°; when liquid begins to boil, lower heat to 350°, cover, leaving air vent open, and cook about 10 minutes, or until fish flakes easily *but is not dry*. Mix 1 tablespoon soft butter with flour, pour cream into fish, and stir in butter-flour mixture. Spoon over fish when thickened, add grapes, shake to heat slightly, and serve immediately. Serves 4 to 5.

SKILLET SHRIMP ORIENTAL

3 tablespoons salad oil
1 clove garlic, minced
½ lb. fresh green beans, bias-cut into 1-inch pieces
1 tablespoon cornstarch
½ teaspoon salt
⅛ teaspoon ginger
2 tablespoons sherry
¾ cup water
1½ lbs. raw shrimp, shelled and deveined
1-inch piece fresh ginger, sliced thin and soaked in 2 tablespoons dry
 sherry (optional)
2 cups hot cooked rice

In electric frying pan, at 325°, heat oil, add garlic and green beans, and sauté for 10 minutes, until glossy, but still very green. Combine cornstarch with salt, ginger, sherry, and water, and add to beans. Stir, add shrimp and fresh ginger, if available, and cook, covered, stirring occasionally, for about 5 minutes, or until shrimp are uniformly pink and sauce has thickened. Serve over hot rice. Serves 4 to 5.

LOBSTER TAIL FRY

2 medium-sized lobster tails
2 eggs
Salt and pepper to taste
1½ cups dry bread crumbs, made in blender
1 cup salad oil
4 tablespoons butter
1 tablespoon lemon juice
4 tablespoons minced fresh parsley

Shell raw lobster tails, and dice meat into 1-inch pieces. Beat eggs, add salt and pepper, and dip-stir lobster pieces into egg mixture. Spread bread crumbs on a flat sheet of foil or waxed paper and roll egg-dipped lobster in crumbs, covering completely. In electric skillet, heat oil to 375°, and quickly cook lobster meat until evenly browned on all sides. In a small pan, over low heat, melt butter, add lemon juice and minced parsley, and blend. Pour over lobster and serve immediately. Serves 3.

SEAFOOD POTPOURRI

½ cup salad oil
4 cloves garlic, minced
4 teaspoons chopped fresh parsley
4 tablespoons flour
6 tablespoons sauterne
2 12-oz. cans chicken broth
2 large lobster tails, cut into 2-inch pieces in shell
1 lb. fresh shrimp, shelled
1 lb. whole fresh scallops, shelled
2 dozen hard-shell clams, in shell, scrubbed and rinsed in several waters

In electric skillet, at 365°, heat oil thoroughly. Add garlic and parsley and fry until brown. Gradually stir in flour until completely blended. Add sauterne and broth and simmer until slightly thickened at 250°. Wash and drain seafood. Add lobster, shrimp, scallops, and clams, and continue to simmer, covered, for 25 minutes, or until clams have opened. Serves 6.

Side Dishes

CELERY CHINOIS

2 tablespoons butter
3 cups celery, cut in ½-inch crescents
½ cup boiling water
2 teaspoons soy sauce
1 teaspoon cornstarch
2 tablespoons cold water
¼ cup almonds, blanched, diced, and toasted

In electric skillet, at 325°, melt butter and add celery, stirring to coat. Add boiling water and soy sauce. Raise temperature to 400°. Bring to a boil. Cover, closing air vent, lower heat to 300°, and simmer for 15 minutes. Stir together cornstarch and cold water until smooth and add to frying pan. Continue to cook, stirring constantly until thickened. Sprinkle with almonds and serve immediately. Serves 4.

SWEET-AND-SOUR POTATOES*

⅓ cup shortening
1 onion, thinly sliced
2 lbs. potatoes, peeled and quartered
1 package (12 ounces) pitted prunes
1 teaspoon salt
1 cup water
⅛ teaspoon sour salt
¼ cup honey

In electric skillet, melt shortening and add onion. Sauté at 325° until golden brown. Add potatoes, brown slightly, then add prunes, salt, and water. Cover, closing air vent, and simmer 1 hour. Add sour salt; mix to dissolve. Add honey and stir. Cover and simmer another 15 minutes, stirring as needed. Serves 4 to 6.

FOIL-WRAPPED POTATOES

6 baking potatoes
3 tablespoons butter
Butter and paprika to taste

Wash and dry potatoes thoroughly. Rub skins with butter. Prick each end of potatoes with a skewer. Wrap individually in aluminum foil. Bake in covered electric frying pan at 375° for 1½ hours. Cut through foil, squeeze potatoes to puff out, and serve with butter and paprika. Serves 6.

CABBAGE ROLLS WITH SAUERKRAUT*

1 large cabbage
2 cups boiled rice
½ lb. sausage meat
2 tablespoons chopped onion
Salt and pepper to taste
1 1-lb. can sauerkraut
4 strips of bacon, cut in quarters

Cook large cabbage in salted boiling water for 3 to 4 minutes. Drain and dry on paper towels. Make filling with rice, sausage meat, onion, salt, and pepper. Fill cabbage leaves and roll, folding in sides over filling, then rolling from one end to the other. Place loose ends down in electric skillet, over thick layer of sauerkraut which has been mixed with the bacon. Add enough hot water to cover sauerkraut. Simmer at 220° for 2 hours, adding more water as needed. Serve with side dish of sour cream. Serves 6 to 8.

PENNSYLVANIA RED CABBAGE*

2 tablespoons bacon drippings
1 medium red cabbage, shredded
2 apples, cored and quartered but not peeled
¼ cup brown sugar
⅓ cup cider vinegar
¼ cup water
1¼ teaspoons salt
Dash pepper
1 teaspoon caraway seeds

In electric skillet, heat bacon drippings at 325°. Add all remaining ingredients, mix, and cover, closing air vent. Cook for 15 minutes if crisp cabbage is desired, or 25 to 30 minutes for soft cabbage. Serves 4 to 6.

FRIED APPLES AND ONIONS*

2 tablespoons butter
2 large onions, peeled and sliced thin
6 large apples, peeled and cut into sections from blossom to stem
1 teaspoon salt
½ teaspoon paprika
½ cup brown sugar
⅛ teaspoon nutmeg

In electric frying pan, melt butter at 320°, add onions, and brown 5 minutes. Place apple sections over onions, and sprinkle with salt, paprika, sugar, and nutmeg. Cover, closing air vent, and simmer at 225° until apples are almost soft. Uncover and continue cooking until apples are soft but do not disintegrate. Serves 6.

APRICOT RICE

¼ cup butter
3 ribs celery, cut into thin crescents
3 tablespoons chopped onion
2 tablespoons apricot preserves
½ teaspoon salt
1½ cups apricot nectar
½ cup water
1 cup uncooked white rice

In electric skillet, melt butter at 300°. Add celery and onion and cook until tender but not brown. Add preserves, salt, nectar, and water. Bring to a boil at 400°, add rice, and cover, closing air vent. Bring to a boil again, cook 5 minutes, then turn off heat, leaving frying pan covered. Let stand 35 minutes, during which rice will absorb all liquid. Rice should be dry and fluffy when done. Serves 4 to 6.

CANDIED SWEET POTATOES*

3 sweet potatoes, unpeeled
¼ lb. butter
½ cup brown sugar
3 tablespoons honey

Boil the potatoes in water to cover, until tender, about 15 minutes. Cool, peel, and slice ½ inch thick. In electric frying pan, at 320°, melt butter, add sugar and honey. Add potatoes and cook, uncovered, gently stirring to keep potatoes covered with syrup. Continue cooking for 20 to 25 minutes, or until well glazed. Serves 4.

CREAMED EGGS ON SPINACH

3 tablespoons butter
3 tablespoons flour
1¾ cups milk
½ teaspoon salt
Dash pepper
½ cup shredded sharp Cheddar cheese
5 hard-boiled eggs, sliced
1 lb. fresh spinach, cooked and drained

In electric frying pan, melt butter at 225°. Blend in flour and gradually add milk, stirring constantly, until thick. Add salt, pepper, and cheese, and stir until melted. Gently add eggs and heat through. Spoon out over hot spinach which has been spread on heated serving platter. Serves 4.

EGGPLANT-SQUASH STEW*

1 large eggplant, unpeeled
2 zucchini, unpeeled
1 green pepper
2 yellow summer squash, unpeeled
1 large onion, diced
¼ cup olive oil
1 cup chili sauce
Juice of 1 lemon
Salt, pepper, garlic powder, oregano, to taste

Cut unpeeled vegetables in 1-inch cubes. Peel onion and cut up. Place oil and vegetables in electric frying pan, at 325°. Sauté, stirring until all pieces are coated. Add chili sauce, lemon, and seasonings and lower heat to 225°, covered, cooking until eggplant is soft, about 1 hour. Serve hot as a vegetable, or cold as an appetizer. Serves 8 to 12, depending on how used.

GARLIC BREAD*

1 loaf French bread, cut in half
¼ pound salted butter
½ teaspoon garlic powder
1 clove garlic, peeled and chopped
1 teaspoon sesame seeds

Cut bread into diagonal slices, but do not cut through to bottom. Place on sheets of aluminum foil which are large enough to cover each half. Melt butter over very low heat. Add garlic powder and chopped garlic and simmer for 15 minutes. With pastry brush, cover slices and brush tops and sides of each half-loaf with garlic butter. Sprinkle with sesame seeds. Wrap each section tightly in foil. Bake in covered electric frying pan at 350° for 30 minutes. Serves 5 to 6.

NOTE: To freeze, combine bread, garlic butter, and sesame seeds, as above, wrap and freeze. When ready to serve, defrost in foil for about 1 hour, and bake as above.

Desserts

BRANDIED PINEAPPLE

2 tablespoons butter
1 can (14 oz.) pineapple chunks
½ cup syrup in which pineapple is packed
2 ounces apricot brandy
½ cup heavy cream

In electric skillet, melt butter at 225° and lightly brown pineapple chunks. Add pineapple syrup and brandy and heat at 350°, uncovered. Shut off heat, cool slightly, and stir in cream. Serves 4 to 5.

FRIED BANANAS

4 tablespoons butter
4 ripe bananas, peeled, split lengthwise, and cut in half
Juice of ½ lemon
3 tablespoons rum
3 tablespoons brown sugar
Dash of salt

In electric frying pan, melt butter at 275°. Place bananas cut-side-down in pan, and sprinkle with lemon juice, rum, and brown sugar. Add dash of salt and cook at 375°, until just golden. Turn once, and cook until easily pierced with fork. Serve warm. Serves 6 to 8.

PINK PEARS

1 1-lb. 13-oz. can Bartlett pear halves, drained
1 6-oz. can whole cranberry sauce

In electric frying pan, place pears cut-side-down, add sauce, and cook both ingredients together at 350° for 20 minutes, spooning sauce over pears periodically. Use as a dessert or as a decorative accompaniment to poultry or meats. Serves 4 to 5.

FRITTER FRUITS*

1 cup all-purpose flour, unsifted
2 teaspoons double-acting baking powder
¼ teaspoon salt
2 tablespoons sugar
2 eggs, beaten
⅓ cup milk
⅓ cup water
2 tablespoons butter, melted
1 banana, sliced
2 apples, peeled, cored, and sliced
½ cup canned pineapple tidbits, drained
½ cup fresh blueberries
6 tablespoons shortening

Sift together flour, baking powder, salt, and sugar. Mix together eggs, milk, water, and melted butter in mixer, and blend in dry ingredients at very slow speed, until just blended. Do not overbeat. Let batter stand at room temperature for 1 hour. Stir fruit into batter and drop by tablespoons into shortening, which has been melted and heated in electric frying pan at 350°. Turn when brown and drain on paper towels. Serve warm, with confectioners' sugar, if desired. Serves 4 to 6.

PANCAKES IN BLUEBERRY SAUCE*

1 cup all-purpose flour, sifted
2 tablespoons sugar
1 teaspoon double-acting baking powder
¼ teaspoon salt
3 eggs, beaten
2 cups skimmed milk
2 tablespoons melted butter, cooled
2 tablespoons shortening

Sift flour, sugar, baking powder and salt together into bowl. Combine eggs, milk, and butter, and add to dry ingredients. Stir just enough to moisten. Heat electric frying pan to 300°. Grease lightly by dipping crumpled paper towel into shortening and brushing cooking surface of frying pan. Repeat with each new batch of batter. Drop level tablespoons of batter near four corners of pan, allowing enough room for batter to spread into uniform round shapes. Cook until rims of pancakes are covered with broken bubbles and underside is golden. Turn with spatula, and brown other side lightly. If preferred, enough batter may be placed in the pan to make one large pancake with each operation, repeating until all batter is used, taking care to keep pancakes thin. When making one large pancake, excess batter may be poured off as soon as base coat begins to set, immediately upon being placed in pan. Yields 24 small or 8 large pancakes. (See p. 228 for sauce.)

BLUEBERRY SAUCE

2 cups fresh blueberries
1 cup water
1 cup sugar
¼ cup frozen orange juice concentrate, undiluted

Heat combined ingredients in electric frying pan at 300°, stirring constantly, until sugar is dissolved. Remove sauce, replace pancakes one at a time in pan, pouring sauce over each pancake. Serves 8.

SUGARED PECANS

1 cup sugar
Dash salt
¼ cup water
¼ cup honey
½ teaspoon vanilla extract
2 cups pecan halves

Mix sugar, salt, water, and honey in electric frying pan and heat at 250° until a little of the mixture dropped in water forms a soft ball. Shut off heat, stir in vanilla and nuts, and continue stirring until thick and creamy. Turn out on waxed paper and separate nuts with two forks. Allow to cool and harden. Serve as confection.

CANDIED GRAPEFRUIT PEEL

Skins of 2 grapefruits, halved
2 cups sugar

Boil grapefruit skins in water to cover for 15 minutes. Drain, add more water and boil again, simmering until skins are very soft. Drain and cool. Scrape all remaining pulp from inside and discard. Cut skins into slivers ½ inch wide by 2½ inches long. Place in electric frying pan, pour sugar over, and heat at 300°, stirring frequently to keep peel coated. When peel begins to crystallize and cook clear, turn out on sugared wax paper and allow to cool and harden. Serve as confection. Yields approximately ½ lb.

COCONUT PEANUT BRITTLE

2 cups sugar
1 cup peanuts, chopped in blender
1 cup shredded coconut
Dash of salt

In electric frying pan, melt sugar at 250°, stirring constantly until it is golden. Remove from heat, add remaining ingredients, and stir just enough to mix together. Pour into shallow greased pan in a thin sheet and allow to cool. When almost cold, break into pieces. Yields approximately 1 lb.

STRAWBERRY SHORTCAKE*

4 tablespoons all-purpose flour, sifted
2 tablespoons cornstarch
1 tablespoon sugar
1 teaspoon baking powder
¼ teaspoon salt
2 tablespoons sweet butter
1 egg
1 lb. strawberries
3 tablespoons sugar
½ pint heavy cream, whipped

Combine dry ingredients. Cream together butter and egg and mix with dry ingredients, to form a soft dough. Pat dough to fit greased 8-inch layer pan. Bake in covered electric frying pan at 350° for 15 minutes. Wash, drain, and hull strawberries and sprinkle with sugar. Reserve a few strawberries for decoration. Fill cooled cake with whipped cream. Decorate with strawberries. Serves 4.

NOTE: For larger cake, double recipe and repeat baking procedure. Spread whipped cream and some strawberries between layers. Use remaining cream and berries to decorate top layer. Doubled recipe serves 8.

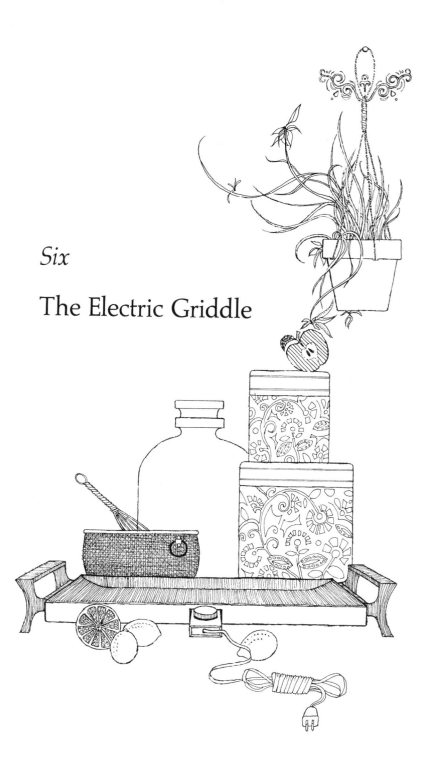

Six

The Electric Griddle

The Electric Griddle

O FTEN THE ELECTRIC GRIDDLE can be used interchangeably with the electric frying pan. However, the griddle's special value is its large cooking surface which allows you to cook many servings at one time or to fry a main course and side dish in one operation. Anyone with children and anyone who likes to entertain will find the electric griddle a wonderfully helpful appliance. You can cook breakfasts and brunches with such ease that you'll find yourself looking forward to special morning meals. Try Cornmeal Griddle Cakes with Orange Applesauce or Farmer's Breakfast or golden French Toast topped with sugar and cinnamon. And of course the griddle is ideal for grilled sandwiches or hamburgers for a crowd. Hot appetizers for a party are a cinch to make on the griddle because the controlled temperature eliminates worry.

The recipes in this chapter are for foods and quantities particularly suited to the griddle. I'm sure you'll soon use many other recipes that take advantage of this marvelous appliance.

Appetizers

POTATO PANCAKES WITH CAVIAR*

3 medium potatoes, grated fine in blender
1 small onion, grated in blender
2 eggs
¼ cup all-purpose flour, sifted
2 teaspoons salt
⅛ teaspoon pepper
3 tablespoons shortening
½ pint sour cream
4 oz. red caviar

Combine potatoes and onions in blender and mix well. Add eggs, flour, salt, and pepper. Preheat electric griddle to 375° and grease well with shortening. Drop mixture by teaspoonfuls on griddle and flatten. Fry slowly, turning once when underside is crisp and brown. Brown second side. Dot each pancake with sour cream and top with ½ teaspoon of red caviar. Serve hot. Serves 12 to 14.

CHEDDAR TRIANGLES*

6 slices day-old white bread, crusts removed
¾ cup milk
3 eggs
6 oz. Cheddar cheese, grated
2 teaspoons ketchup
2 teaspoons flour
1 teaspoon paprika
4 tablespoons butter

Soak bread in milk, turning once. Beat eggs and add cheese, ketchup, flour, and paprika. Mix well. Spread half the cheese mixture on one side of soaked bread. Grease full surface of griddle with butter and place bread cheese-side-down, frying at 325° until golden brown. Spread remaining cheese on top of each slice. Turn, and continue frying until second side is golden brown. Cut each slice into 4 triangles and serve hot. Serves 8 to 10.

CHICKEN PINWHEELS*

1 cup cooked chicken meat, chopped fine in blender
1 egg
2 tablespoons blender-chopped onion
2 tablespoons blender-chopped celery
1 tablespoon mayonnaise
1 tablespoon prepared mustard
6 slices of white bread, crusts removed

Combine all ingredients except bread. Spread bread slices with mixture and roll up. Wrap each roll tightly in waxed paper and refrigerate overnight. When ready to serve, slice each roll into ½-inch pinwheels. Grease griddle and heat to 350°. Fry pinwheels until browned, turning once. Serve hot. Serves 12.

MINIATURE FISH CAKES*

2 slices bread, crusts removed
¼ cup milk
1 lb. fish fillets, cooked
½ teaspoon salt
½ teaspoon thyme
1 tablespoon Worcestershire sauce
1 tablespoon lemon juice
½ teaspoon parsley flakes
1 tablespoon baking powder
1 egg, beaten
½ cup seasoned bread crumbs

Break bread into pieces and soak in milk. Mix with remaining ingredients and shape into miniature cakes, about 1 inch in diameter. Roll in bread crumbs. Fry on greased griddle at 325° until golden on both sides, turning only once. Serve with horseradish sauce. Serves 10.

HORSERADISH SAUCE

2 teaspoons dry mustard
2 teaspoons white vinegar
4 tablespoons prepared horseradish
1 tablespoon sugar
½ teaspoon salt
½ pint sour cream

Combine dry mustard and vinegar. Add remaining ingredients and stir.

SHRIMP PUFFS*

2 lbs. uncooked shrimp, peeled and deveined
3 eggs, separated
3 tablespoons flour
½ teaspoon salt
¼ teaspoon paprika
3 tablespoons cold milk

Beat egg yolks in electric mixer until thick and lemon colored. Add flour, seasonings, and milk. Beat until smooth. Whip egg whites until stiff and fold into yolk mixture. Grease griddle and preheat to 325°. Drop teaspoon of egg mixture, top with 1 uncooked shrimp, then cover with another teaspoon of egg mixture. Cook until browned on one side, turn only once and brown second side. Serves 12.

MINIATURE GRIDDLE SANDWICHES

PIZZA GRILLED CHEESE

8 slices white bread, crusts removed
4 oz. sharp Cheddar cheese
4 tablespoons tomato paste
1 teaspoon oregano
1 teaspoon garlic powder
Dash of cayenne pepper
1 teaspoon onion flakes
1 teaspoon salt
Dash pepper
½ cup butter, melted

On each of 4 slices of bread, place 1-oz. slice of cheese. Spread tomato paste over it, and sprinkle with one-fourth of the seasonings, which have been mixed together. Cover with remaining 4 slices of bread, and brush outside of sandwiches top and bottom with melted butter. Sauté on preheated griddle at 375° in remaining butter until golden on both sides and cheese appears melted. Cut each sandwich into 4 triangles, and serve hot. Serves 6 to 8.

HAM SALAD

6 slices white bread, crusts removed
½ cup cooked ham, chopped
2 hard-boiled eggs, chopped
1 teaspoon Worcestershire sauce
2 tablespoons mayonnaise
1 tablespoon prepared mustard
¼ cup melted butter

On each of 3 slices of bread, spread remaining ingredients which have been combined, except butter. Cover with remaining 3 slices of bread, and brush outside of sandwiches on top and bottom with melted butter. Sauté on preheated griddle at 375° in remaining butter until golden on both sides. Cut each sandwich into 4 triangles and serve hot. Serves 4 to 6.

MEAT AND CHEESE

4 ounces blue cheese
4 ounces cream cheese
6 tablespoons milk
8 slices white bread, crusts removed
12 slices chipped beef
2 eggs, beaten
¼ cup milk
¼ teaspoon salt
4 tablespoons butter

Cream together blue cheese, cream cheese, and milk. Spread 4 bread slices. Place 3 slices of chipped beef on top of each sandwich, then top again with cheese mixture. Cover with remaining 4 slices of bread. Cut each sandwich into 4 triangles. Mix together eggs, milk, and salt, and dip each of the 16 triangles in egg mixture, turning over to soak top and bottom. Grease griddle with butter and preheat to 375°. Fry triangles, turning once to brown both sides. Serves 6 to 8.

STUFFED BACON ROLL-UPS

½ lb. bacon slices, cut in half
About 20 stuffed green olives

Wrap each half bacon slice around green olive and secure with wooden toothpick. Fry on preheated, ungreased griddle at 350° until crisp. Serves 8.

Main Dishes

FRIED LIVER AND BACON

2 lbs. calves' liver
8 strips bacon
Salt and pepper to taste
½ cup flour
¼ teaspoon paprika
1 medium onion, sliced and separated into rings

Cut veins from liver, cut into serving pieces, and wash. Dry with paper towels. Place bacon on griddle and set at 350°. Cook until bacon is crisp, turning once. Remove and drain on paper towels. Reserve 3 tablespoons of bacon fat in griddle. Season liver and coat with flour to which paprika has been added. Raise griddle temperature to 375°. Quickly fry liver on both sides, until crisp on outside but not dry—a total of about 5 minutes. When liver has been turned, add onion slices and fry alongside, adding more fat if needed. Return bacon to griddle at last minute, then serve immediately, decorating liver with bacon strips and onion rings. Serves 8.

BEEF POTATO PATTIES*

1½ cups mashed potatoes
1 egg
1 tablespoon minced onion
¼ teaspoon paprika
1 teaspoon salt
¼ teaspoon pepper
1½ lbs. ground chuck
1 teaspoon salt
¼ teaspoon pepper
¼ teaspoon garlic powder
1 slice white bread, crust removed
¼ cup milk
1 egg
½ carrot, grated

Mix mashed potatoes with egg, minced onion, paprika, salt, and pepper. Mix ground beef with salt, pepper, garlic powder, bread which has been soaked in milk, remainder of milk, egg, and grated carrot. Place meat mixture between two sheets of waxed paper and roll or press into 1-inch-thick rectangle. Remove top sheet of waxed paper. Spread potato mixture over meat, and roll up in jelly-roll fashion. Discard bottom sheet of waxed paper. Wrap in waxed paper and chill. Freezer may be used for quick chilling. To cook, remove waxed paper, and slice roll into 1-inch circles. Fry on preheated, greased griddle at 350°, turning once, until meat is no longer pink and patties are golden brown. Serves 8.

BLUE CHEESE HAMBURGERS*

2 lbs. ground chuck
2 oz. blue cheese, crumbled
1 tablespoon chopped onion
1 teaspoon prepared horseradish
1 teaspoon prepared mustard
1 tablespoon ketchup
1 teaspoon salt
Dash pepper

Combine all ingredients. Form into 8 patties about ¾ inch thick. Cook on ungreased griddle at 325° until well browned, turning once. Serve on toasted hamburger buns. Serves 8.

BREADED PORK CHOPS WITH APPLE RINGS*

3 lbs. center cut pork chops, ½ inch thick
½ cup flour
1 teaspoon salt
Dash pepper
2 eggs, beaten
1 cup dry, seasoned bread crumbs
3 large apples, unpeeled, cored, and cut in ½-inch rings
¼ cup brown sugar
¼ teaspoon cinnamon

Dredge pork chops in flour which has been seasoned with salt and pepper. Dip in beaten eggs, and roll in bread crumbs. Cook on lightly greased, preheated griddle at 350°, 5 minutes on each side. Turn heat down to 300° and continue cooking for 45 minutes more, turning several times. During last 15 minutes of cooking, dip apple rings in brown sugar and cinnamon and add to one side of griddle, greasing slightly if necessary. Cook apples until brown and tender, and serve over pork chops. Serves 6.

HAM FRITTERS*

1 lb. smoked ham, ground
1 lb. ground pork
2 eggs, beaten
¾ cup milk
1 cup fresh bread crumbs
1 teaspoon salt
Dash pepper
2 tablespoons chopped onion
¼ cup ketchup
1 cup dry, seasoned bread crumbs
1 cup cranberry sauce

Mix together ham and pork. Combine eggs, milk, fresh bread crumbs, salt, pepper, onion, and ketchup. Let stand until bread is soft, then add to meat mixture. Shape into ½-inch-thick patties, roll in seasoned bread crumbs, and fry on greased griddle at 350° to brown on both sides—about 5 minutes. Turn down heat to 300° and continue cooking for 45 minutes more, turning frequently. Serve with cranberry sauce. Serves 8.

VEAL CUTLETS VIENNESE*

8 6-oz. veal cutlets
Salt and pepper to taste
½ cup flour
3 eggs
2 teaspoons water
2 cups fine, dry bread crumbs
¼ lb. butter
2 lemons

Flatten veal cutlets with wooden mallet between pieces of waxed paper. Sprinkle with salt and pepper and dip in flour. Beat eggs with water. Dip veal in egg and then in bread crumbs, patting crumbs down with flat surface of knife. Melt butter on griddle at 350° and add meat, cooking until golden brown. Cook about 15 minutes, turning over once. Serve with lemon wedges. Serves 8.

VEAL CUTLETS WITH HAM AND CHEESE*

12 6-oz. veal cutlets, pounded thin
Salt and pepper to taste
6 slices Swiss cheese, ⅛ inch thick
6 thin slices baked or boiled ham
½ cup flour
3 eggs, beaten
2 cups fine, dry bread crumbs, seasoned
¼ lb. butter

Sprinkle meat with salt and pepper. Trim cheese and ham slices to be somewhat smaller than veal cutlets. Place one slice of each on each of 6 cutlets and cover with remaining cutlets. Cut in half. Press edges together, and dip in flour, covering both sides. Dip in egg and bread crumbs. Melt butter on griddle at 350°, add meat, and cook 10 to 15 minutes on each side, or until uniformly golden. Serves 8 to 12.

CLAM PANCAKES*

1 cup all-purpose flour, sifted
½ teaspoon salt
1 cup milk
2 eggs
¼ cup vegetable shortening, melted

FILLING

1 7-oz. can minced clams, drained
1 egg, beaten
1 cup ricotta cheese
¼ teaspoon garlic powder
1 pint sour cream

Mix flour and salt in electric mixer bowl. Add milk, and beat with mixer until smooth. Add eggs, and beat thoroughly. Add melted shortening and mix well. Bake on ungreased griddle at 375°, allowing ½ cup batter for each large pancake. Turn when large bubbles appear on surface and edges are slightly brown, and cook until second side is brown. Mix all filling ingredients except sour cream and place some of the mixture in center of each pancake. Roll up and place pancakes close together in shallow baking dish. Heat in 350° oven for 20 minutes. Serve with sour cream. Serves 8.

FILLET OF FLOUNDER AMANDINE*

2 lbs. fillet of flounder
Salt and pepper to taste
Dash of nutmeg
1 egg
1 tablespoon milk
1 cup fine, dry bread crumbs
6 tablespoons cooking oil
½ cup blender-chopped, blanched almonds
½ cup coarsely chopped onion
½ cup butter
1 tablespoon lemon juice

Preheat griddle to 350°. Season flounder fillets. Dip in egg which has been beaten with milk. Roll in bread crumbs. Heat cooking oil. Fry fish on griddle, allowing 5 minutes for each side, turning once. Combine chopped nuts and chopped onion in small saucepan and cook in butter until lightly browned. Add lemon juice and pour over fish. Serves 6.

SWORDFISH IN GARLIC*

2 lbs. swordfish steaks, 1 inch thick
Salt and pepper to taste
1 clove garlic, minced
¼ cup butter, softened
Juice of 1 lemon

Season fish with salt and pepper. Mix minced garlic into softened butter, and spread on top and bottom of fish steaks. Preheat griddle to 350° and fry steak 8 to 10 minutes on each side, turning once. Pour lemon juice over fish. Serves 6.

SEA SQUAB IN BACON*

2 lbs. sea squab, or blowfish
1 cup fine, dry bread crumbs, seasoned with salt, pepper, and dill weed
½ lb. bacon slices, cut in half

Toss washed but not dried fish in seasoned bread crumbs. Wrap each fish in ½ strip of bacon, and place with bacon ends facing down on ungreased griddle. Fry about 10 minutes on each side at 350°, or until bacon is crisp and brown. Serves 6.

Side Dishes

GRILLED TOMATO SLICES

¼ cup butter
6 large, firm tomatoes, sliced ½ inch thick
Salt and pepper to taste
½ cup flour
¼ cup grated Parmesan cheese

Melt butter on griddle at 300°. Sprinkle tomatoes with salt and pepper and dip in flour. Fry on griddle about 3 to 4 minutes on one side. Turn, sprinkle browned top with Parmesan cheese, and cook another 3 minutes, until underside is brown. Serves 6.

WESTERN EGG SCRAMBLE

8 oz. brown-and-serve precooked sausage
8 eggs
½ cup milk
1 teaspoon salt
Dash pepper
¼ cup blender-chopped green pepper
¼ cup blender-chopped green onion
¼ cup blender-chopped pimiento

Brown sausages on griddle at 350°. Reduce heat to 320°. Beat together eggs, milk, salt, and pepper. Pour over sausages. Sprinkle vegetables on top. With fork, gather cooked edges toward center, allowing uncooked egg to run off to outer edges. Continue cooking until eggs are cooked through but still glossy and moist, or according to preference. Serves 4 to 6.

FARMER'S BREAKFAST

4 tablespoons butter
½ cup diced, cooked ham
4 cold, cooked potatoes, sliced
¼ cup chopped onion
8 eggs
½ cup milk
1 teaspoon salt
Dash pepper

Melt butter on griddle at 350°. Spread ham, potatoes, and onion on griddle and brown without stirring. Beat together eggs and milk and season with salt and pepper. Pour over browned potato mixture and stir until eggs are done. Serves 4 to 6.

BACON AND CHUTNEY*

½ lb. bacon
10 oz. mango chutney
8 slices toast, cut into points

Place bacon on cold griddle and set at 350°. Fry until bacon is crisp, turning several times. Drain on paper towels. Crumble bacon into chutney and serve spread on toast points for breakfast or as appetizer. Serves 6 to 10, depending on how used.

BRAIN PATTIES*

2 lbs. calves' brains
1 teaspoon salt
Dash pepper
¼ cup flour
2 eggs
4 tablespoons butter

Cook brains in boiling water until all traces of pink disappear. Drain. Cool until easily handled, then remove all membranes. Mix with remaining ingredients, except butter. Melt butter in griddle at 350° and spread. Drop batter by tablespoonfuls and fry until golden on both sides, turning once. Serve with applesauce, sour cream and caviar, plain as a luncheon dish, or in smaller patties as appetizer. Serves 8 to 14, depending on how used.

SWEET POTATO CAKES*

1½ cups mashed sweet potatoes
Salt and pepper to taste
2 tablespoons melted butter
1 tablespoon maple syrup
1 egg, separated
¼ cup flour
1 tablespoon water
½ cup fine, dry bread crumbs
4 tablespoons butter
1 cup whole cranberry sauce

Mix together potatoes, salt and pepper, melted butter, and maple syrup. Add egg yolk. Form potato patties, using a tablespoon of mixture to ensure uniformity of size. Roll each patty in flour. Mix egg white with water, dip cakes in this mixture, and then roll in bread crumbs. Melt butter on griddle at 350°, and fry cakes until crisp and brown. Serve with cranberry sauce. Serves 8.

EGGPLANT PIZZA*

1 medium eggplant
¼ cup flour
1 egg, beaten
1 tablespoon milk
½ cup fine, dry bread crumbs, seasoned
4 tablespoons cooking oil
1 teaspoon salt
⅛ teaspoon pepper
1 teaspoon oregano
2 tablespoons chopped parsley
¼ cup grated Parmesan cheese
6 slices mozzarella cheese
1 8-oz. can tomato sauce

Peel and slice eggplant in ½-inch slices. Dredge with flour. Thin egg with milk, dip eggplant, then roll in bread crumbs. Heat cooking oil in griddle to 375° and brown eggplant on both sides. Remove from griddle and drain on paper towels. Place eggplant in 10 x 6 x 1½-inch baking dish. Sprinkle with salt, pepper, oregano, chopped parsley, and Parmesan cheese. Top with mozzarella. Cover with tomato sauce and bake in moderate oven at 350° about 20 minutes, until sauce bubbles and cheese is melted. Serves 6.

YOGURT PANCAKES*

4 tablespoons butter
2 cups unflavored yogurt
2 eggs, beaten
8 tablespoons all-purpose flour
2 teaspoons baking powder

Melt butter in griddle at 300°. Mix yogurt with remaining ingredients and drop by tablespoonfuls on griddle. Fry until golden on both sides, turning only once. Serve with jam or sugar, or plain as a side dish with meat or fish. Serves 4.

Desserts

BANANA PATTIES*

2 cups all-purpose flour, sifted
⅓ cup sugar
1 tablespoon baking powder
1 teaspoon salt
½ teaspoon cardamom
½ cup finely chopped almonds
1 egg, beaten
1¼ cups milk
5 firm bananas, peeled and cut into ½-inch diagonal slices
6 tablespoons vegetable shortening

Sift together flour, sugar, baking powder, salt, and cardamom. Stir in chopped almonds. Combine egg and milk. Add liquid all at once to flour mixture, stirring until well blended to make medium-thick batter. Stir in banana slices, making sure they are well covered. Melt half the shortening on griddle at 350°, and spread to cover surface. Drop 2 tablespoons of batter for each patty, spacing to allow for spreading during cooking. When golden on underside, add remaining shortening and turn, frying until golden. Serves 8 to 10.

GRIDDLE CRÊPES À L'ORANGE*

6 eggs
6 tablespoons flour
Pinch of salt
1 teaspoon sugar
¾ cup milk
3 tablespoons butter

Beat together eggs, flour, salt, sugar, and milk to make batter the consistency of light cream. (Add a bit more milk, if needed.) Grease griddle by rubbing on some of the butter with paper towel, repeating with each new batch of batter. Heat to 325°. Pour batter onto griddle, using two tablespoonfuls per crêpe and allowing it to spread thin. Brown lightly on both sides and keep warm in heating tray until all batter has been used. Serve with flaming orange sauce (see recipe below).

ORANGE SAUCE

1 orange
1 lemon
6 lumps of sugar
⅛ lb. butter, soft
⅛ lb. butter
2 oz. Grand Marnier liqueur
½ cup brandy

Rub lumps of sugar over unpeeled orange and unpeeled lemon to absorb flavor and oils from the fruit. Squeeze orange. Soften the sugar with orange juice, and cream with butter. Set aside. In shallow flameproof serving dish, melt butter and stir in Grand Marnier. Add orange butter and heat. Dip crêpes in this and roll up in the dish. When ready to serve, heat brandy, pour over crêpes, and ignite. Place on serving plates, spoon flaming sauce over crêpes, and serve immediately. Serves 6.

FRENCH TOAST*

3 eggs, beaten
½ cup milk
¾ teaspoon sugar
¼ teaspoon salt
2 teaspoons vanilla extract
6 slices white bread, with crust
3 tablespoons butter

Beat together eggs, milk, sugar, and salt. Stir in vanilla. Place in shallow bowl which will accommodate slices of bread easily, and soak bread slices one by one, turning once. Melt half the butter on griddle at 325°, and spread to cover surface. Fry bread until golden, add remaining butter, turn once, and fry until evenly golden on both sides. Serve with jam or sugar and cinnamon. Serves 4 to 6.

CORNMEAL GRIDDLE CAKES*

¾ cup cornmeal
2 tablespoons molasses
1 teaspoon salt
2 eggs
1½ cups milk
1¼ cups all-purpose flour, sifted
3 teaspoons baking powder
2 tablespoons melted butter
3 tablespoons butter

Mix cornmeal, molasses, and salt. Beat eggs and add. Add milk. Sift together flour and baking powder and add. Pour in melted butter and blend. Grease griddle with half the remaining butter, pour in batter, using about ¼ cup for each pancake, and brown at 350°. Add remaining butter, turn, and bake until golden. Serve with orange applesauce (see recipe below). Serves 8 to 10.

ORANGE APPLESAUCE

6 large apples, peeled, cored, and cut into pieces
¼ cup light brown sugar
2 tablespoons grated orange rind
2 tablespoons orange juice

In covered saucepan, on low heat, cook together apples and brown sugar until soft. Remove from heat, stir in orange rind and juice, and serve immediately with griddle cakes.

GRILLED PEACHES

3 tablespoons butter
12 canned peach halves (two 1-lb. 13-oz. cans)
½ cup blanched almonds, finely chopped in blender
1 teaspoon almond extract
½ teaspoon grated orange rind
12 ladyfingers, broken in small bits
¼ cup dark brown sugar
¼ cup muscatel wine

Preheat griddle to 300° and melt butter. Place peach halves round-side-down on griddle and fry to brown lightly. Combine nuts, extract, orange rind, ladyfingers, brown sugar, and wine, and shape into 12 balls the size of a peach pit. Place filling in peach cavities, flattening to fill completely. Turn peaches, filled-side-down, and continue frying for about 5 minutes, or until browned. Serves 6.

FRIED CHEESE CAKES*

2 lbs. farmer cheese
4 eggs, beaten
6 tablespoons flour
½ teaspoon salt
2 tablespoons sugar
3 tablespoons butter

Crumble farmer cheese; stir in eggs, flour, salt, and sugar. Butter griddle and preheat to 300°. Drop batter by tablespoonfuls and brown, turning once, about 5 minutes on each side. Serve hot with jam or sour cream and sugar. Serves 10 to 12.

NOTE: This batter may be dropped by tablespoonfuls into boiling water until dumplings rise to the top. They may be served, as above, after just being boiled, or may be boiled first and then lightly fried in butter on griddle until golden.

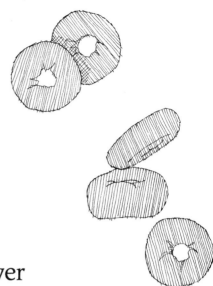

Seven

The Deep Fryer

The Deep Fryer

THERE'S NO QUESTION that having a deep fryer is a luxury, especially in our diet-conscious era, but it has a number of assets that make it a very useful appliance. We all have favorite fried foods—who could give up fried chicken or French fried onions?—and by cooking them in this controlled-heat appliance, they can be made as crisp and greaseless as possible. Furthermore, this deep pot is very useful for cooking pot roasts, stews, and fricassées. And I often use mine for preparing soups. A sample of recipes is included here. Others may be found throughout the book.

The electric fryer is a pleasure to cook with. It maintains an even, constant temperature that eliminates the usual hazards of smoking or burning. Because it fries foods at the proper temperature, you can usually reuse shortening many times. There are some instances when fat must be discarded after only one use, but the dividends in flavor compensate. For the sake of economy in the use of shortening, the recipes in this chapter are arranged so as to indicate which foods allow fat to be reused and which do not.

The recipes that follow, combined with your own family favorites, offer a marvelous opportunity to use your fryer to its fullest economical and palate-tempting advantage. Just remember two rules: Always preheat fat to required temperature before beginning to cook, and always drain fried foods thoroughly on absorbent paper before serving.

For Reusable Fat

Appetizers

CHEESE MORES

¼ lb. caraway cheese, grated in blender
1 teaspoon prepared mustard
1 teaspoon prepared horseradish
1 cup pancake mix
¾ cup milk

Combine cheese, mustard, and horseradish, and blend. Shape into
¾-inch balls. Make batter by combining pancake flour with milk.
Add cheese balls a few at a time and coat thoroughly. Lift out with
slotted spoon and drop into deep, hot fat which has been heated
in deep fryer to 360°. Fry until just golden, turning over once,
about ½ minute. Drain on absorbent paper. Serves 12.

CHEESE PUFFS

2¼ cups flour
½ teaspoon salt
1 cup beer
4 egg whites, stiffly beaten
12 1-oz. wedges of processed Swiss Gruyère cheese) (2 packages)

Mix flour and salt with beer. Let stand at least 4 hours in warm place. Fold in beaten egg whites. Cut each cheese triangle in half. Dip into batter and fry in hot deep fat at 350° until golden, about 2 minutes. Drain on absorbent paper. Serves 8 to 12.

FRENCH-FRIED RAVIOLI

PASTRY

1½ cups sifted flour
1 teaspoon salt
1 egg
3 tablespoons water
Cornstarch

Sift flour and salt into bowl. Beat egg with water and add to flour. Work into dough, adding more water if necessary. Turn out on floured board and knead smooth. Cover with damp towel. Let rest 30 minutes. Rub board with cornstarch. Roll dough very thin, about ⅛ inch thick. Cut into 2½-inch squares.

FILLING

½ **lb. chopped beef, pork, or chicken**
1 small onion, finely chopped in blender
2 tablespoons butter
2 teaspoons soy sauce
1 teaspoon salt
¼ **teaspoon garlic powder**
½ **teaspoon oregano**
Dash pepper

Combine meat and onion and sauté in butter, until lightly browned. Combine with seasonings and drop by teaspoonfuls into 2-inch pastry squares. Moisten edges of pastry and bring together diagonal corners, making a triangle. Bring opposite corners together, moisten and press together. Fry in deep fat in basket at 365° until brown. Serves 10 to 12.

Main Dishes

BATTER-FRIED CHICKEN

3 2-lb. broilers, disjointed into small pieces
1 egg, beaten
¾ **cup milk**
1 cup all-purpose flour, sifted
½ **teaspoon salt**
½ **teaspoon garlic powder**

Wash chicken and dry well. Beat remaining ingredients together in electric mixer or blender. Dip chicken pieces one at a time, drain, and fry in deep fat at 350° until well browned, about 10 minutes. Drain on absorbent paper. Serves 8.

CHICKEN KIEV*

6 whole chicken breasts, boned
½ lb. sweet butter
2 cloves garlic, crushed
4 teaspoons chopped chives
¾ cup all-purpose flour
Salt and pepper to taste
2 eggs, beaten
¾ cup bread crumbs

Cut chicken breasts in half. Flatten breasts between layers of waxed paper with mallet. Fill each breast half with ⅙ of the butter and some of the garlic and chives. Roll chicken around butter and fasten with wooden toothpick, making sure all the butter is covered. Dust with seasoned flour; roll in egg and then in bread crumbs. Fry in deep fat at 360°, until golden, about 3 to 5 minutes. Drain, place on cookie sheet in hot oven, and bake at 425° for 5 minutes. Serve very hot to allow butter to spurt from the cutlets when cut open. Serves 6.

NOTE: This may be frozen when assembled and breaded, but not fried. When ready to serve, fry without prior defrosting, allowing double the cooking time.

MARUSIA'S PIROSHKI*

DOUGH

1 cup milk, heated to lukewarm
1 package dry active yeast
4 cups all-purpose flour, sifted
¼ lb. butter
1 tablespoon salad oil
Pinch salt
1 teaspoon sugar
3 egg yolks
1 jigger vodka or brandy

Dissolve yeast in half the warm milk, stirring to dissolve fully. Let stand 10 minutes. Add 2 cups of flour, and when evenly mixed, cover with clean towel and allow to stand at room temperature for ½ hour. Dough will rise. Meanwhile, mix butter with oil, salt, sugar, and egg yolks. Gradually add remaining warm milk. Add vodka. Stir in remaining flour. Combine with risen yeast dough and cover, allowing to rise in a warm place for 1 to 2 hours.

FILLING

1 medium onion, chopped fine
1 tablespoon butter
1½ lbs. ground chuck
3 chicken livers
1 egg, hard-boiled and chopped
1 teaspoon finely chopped fresh dill
1 teaspoon salt
⅛ teaspoon pepper

Brown onion in butter; add meat and chicken livers and brown. Stir in chopped hard-boiled egg and seasonings. Pinch off pieces of dough and roll into 1½-inch balls. Place on floured surface, flour hands, and flatten and stretch each ball of dough to form flat oval surface. Place 1 teaspoon of filling in center, fold over lengthwise, and pinch edges together. Turn with pinched side down and place on floured board, shaping into oblong oval with hands. Cover with clean towel and allow to rest and rise at least another ½ hour. Heat fat in deep fryer to 360°, and drop in piroshki one at a time until surface is covered. Do not crowd. When golden on one side, they will usually turn over by themselves. If not, turn over until uniformly golden on all sides. Drain on absorbent paper. Makes about 30, to serve 10 to 16.

NOTE: These may be frozen after deep-frying and reheated when ready to serve by refrying briefly in deep fat, or by placing on cookie sheet in hot oven at 350° for approximately 30 to 40 minutes.

Side Dishes

CHINESE FRIED NOODLES

1 lb. medium egg noodles
½ lb. ground beef
2 tablespoons butter
Soy sauce to taste
2 slices cooked ham

Boil noodles 5 minutes, drain, and then fry in deep fat at 325° until golden crisp. Cook ground beef in butter, stirring frequently. Add a little water and soy sauce to make gravy. Serve noodles topped with sauce and thin strips of ham. Serves 4 to 5.

MASHED POTATO PUFFS*

3 cups seasoned mashed potatoes (leftovers are fine)
2 eggs
2 tablespoons flour
1 tablespoon melted butter
½ tablespoon baking powder
2 tablespoons grated Parmesan cheese

Combine all ingredients in the order listed. Heat shortening to 400°, and drop in potato batter in rounded tablespoonfuls. Fry until browned. Serves 6.

SWEET POTATO BITES*

7 sweet potatoes
1 egg, beaten
7 apples
1 cup brown sugar
4 tablespoons cornstarch
½ cup orange juice
¾ teaspoon salt
¼ teaspoon nutmeg
1 teaspoon grated orange rind

Boil sweet potatoes until just tender. Peel and mash. Blend in beaten egg. Dice peeled apples into small cubes and add to mashed potatoes. Combine sugar, cornstarch, orange juice, and seasonings, and bring to a boil until thickened. Add orange rind; then combine with apple and potato mixture. Drop into hot fat, about 375°, from rounded tablespoonfuls, and cook 5 minutes. Serves 8.

CORN FRITTERS*

6 fresh ears of corn
¼ cup flour
½ teaspoon salt
⅛ teaspoon pepper
1 egg, lightly beaten
2 tablespoons cottage cheese

Cut the corn off the cob by splitting each row of kernels lengthwise with point of sharp knife and then shaving kernels off cob. Scrape remaining corn off cob with spoon. Mix with remaining ingredients and drop by teaspoonfuls into 365° fat. Cook until golden, turning once. Drain on absorbent paper, and serve hot. Serves 6.

FRENCH-FRIED ONIONS*

4 large onions
1 cup milk
1 cup water
1 cup flour

Slice onions into very thin rings and soak in mixture of milk and water, making sure to cover. If mixture is insufficient, add more milk and water in equal proportions. Let stand at least 30 minutes. Drain. Dredge with flour, tossing lightly to make sure all rings are covered. Place in fryer basket. Fry in deep fat at 360° until golden. Drain on absorbent paper. Serves 6.

Desserts

HOT IRON PATTIES*

NOTE: A patty iron must be used. This long-handled iron mold
is heated in the fat, then immersed in batter and returned to the
hot fat. As the batter cooks, it expands and drops off the iron.

½ **cup evaporated milk**
½ **cup water**
1 **teaspoon sugar**
½ **teaspoon salt**
1 **egg, unbeaten**
1 **cup sifted flour**

Combine milk, water, sugar, salt, and egg. Stir in flour; then beat
until smooth. (Blender may be used to mix batter.) Heat shortening to 365°. Heat patty iron by dipping in hot shortening for about
15 seconds. Dip into batter, not immersing over the top. Dip in hot
fat and lift out patty iron when shell has browned slightly and is
ready to slip off. Turn patty shell to brown other side. Drain on
absorbent paper. Serve shells filled with creamed meat, fish, or
vegetables, using a basic white sauce as the base, or any variation
you may desire. Serves 10 to 12.

RICOTTA PUFFS*

1 lb. ricotta cheese
3 eggs, lightly beaten
4 teaspoons baking powder
2 tablespoons sugar
1/16 teaspoon salt
1 cup flour

Mix all ingredients in the order given, gradually adding the flour, and allow to stand 1 hour. Heat fat to 360°. Drop batter by rounded teaspoonfuls and fry 3 to 5 minutes. Turn once. Drain on absorbent paper. Dust with sugar. Serve with sour cream, ice cream, or applesauce. Serves 6.

CHERRY FRITTERS*

1 cup sifted flour
½ cup sugar
2 teaspoons baking powder
1 teaspoon salt
2 eggs, beaten
⅓ cup milk
2 teaspoons shortening, melted
1 cup pitted sour cherries

Sift together flour, sugar, baking powder, and salt. In blender, combine egg, milk, and melted shortening, and pour into dry ingredients. Stir until smooth. Stir in cherries. Batter is medium thick —do not thin. Drop by teaspoonfuls into deep fat at 350° for 3 to 5 minutes. Serve immediately to retain crispness. Serves 6 to 8.

BOWKNOTS*

6 egg yolks
¼ cup sugar
1 tablespoon melted butter
⅓ cup heavy cream, whipped
½ teaspoon vanilla
2 cups flour
½ teaspoon salt

Beat egg yolks until thick. Add sugar and beat. Stir in butter. Fold in whipped cream and vanilla. Sift together flour and salt, and add to yolk mixture to make soft dough. Chill well. Divide in half and roll each piece ⅛-inch thick. Cut in 3 x ¾-inch strips. Cut a slit lengthwise in center of each and pull one end through. Fry a few at a time at 375° about 1½ minutes, or until golden. Drain on absorbent paper. While warm, sift confectioners' sugar over knots. Makes about 60 cookies.

ROSETTES*

Requires patty iron, in rosette shape. (See directions for Hot Iron Patties, p. 269.)

2 eggs
1 tablespoon sugar
¼ teaspoon salt
1 cup sifted flour
1 cup milk
1 teaspoon vanilla

Combine eggs, sugar, and salt. Beat well. Add flour, milk, and vanilla. Beat until smooth. Heat rosette in fat at 375°. Dip in batter just to rim, then immediately in hot fat. When browning, pastry rosette will fall off iron. Turn over to brown on other side. Lift out. Drain on absorbent paper. Tip iron upside down to drain. Reheat iron before making next rosette. Sprinkle with confectioners' sugar. Makes about 60 cookies.

GERMAN DOUGHNUTS*

1 medium potato, peeled and sliced
2 cups salted water
1 cup sugar
2 eggs, well beaten
1 teaspoon salt
¼ cup shortening
1 package dry active yeast
¼ cup warm water
6 cups sifted all-purpose flour

Cook potato in salted water until tender. Drain, reserving 1½ cups potato water. Mash potato and measure ¼ cupful. Beat with sugar in large mixing bowl until well blended. Add well-beaten eggs. Add salt and shortening. Add hot potato water until shortening is dissolved and mixture smooth. Let cool to lukewarm. Dissolve yeast in warm water until bubbly. Beat into mixture. Stir in flour gradually. Dough will be soft. Knead on floured surface until elastic and smooth. Place in greased bowl. Cover and let rise in warm place until double in bulk, about 2 to 3 hours. Turn onto floured board and knead several times. Divide into sections and roll to thickness of about ⅓ inch. Cut donuts with donut cutter. Place on pans that have been slightly greased. Cover and let rise a second time, about 1 hour. Fry in deep fat at 375°, about 2 minutes on each side. Drain, and sprinkle with sugar, cinnamon, or confectioners' sugar. Makes 4 dozen.

FRYER TWISTS*

2 eggs, slightly beaten
6 tablespoons milk
½ teaspoon vanilla
3 tablespoons sugar
3¼ cups sifted flour
½ teaspoon salt
1 tablespoon salad oil

Mix all ingredients. Roll out on floured surface very thinly. Cut into squares. Make a cut in one corner of each square; pull opposite corner through. Fry in hot fat at 375° until golden, about 2 minutes, turning once. Drain on absorbent paper and sprinkle with confectioners' sugar. Serves 20.

For Fat That Must Be Discarded After Use

Appetizers

CHICKEN LIVER RUMAKI WITH WATER CHESTNUTS*

12 chicken livers, cut in half
1 can water chestnuts
24 strips bacon
3 tablespoons soy sauce, seasoned with dash pepper and garlic powder

Slice each chicken liver half partially through. Slice water chestnuts into flat discs. Dip livers in seasoned soy sauce, insert a slice of water chestnut between layers of liver and tightly wrap a strip of bacon around it, fastening with wooden toothpick. Deep-fry at 365° until bacon is crisp. Serve immediately after draining, or reheat in oven on ungreased cookie sheet just before serving. Serves 10 to 12.

BATTER-FRIED SHRIMP*

3 lbs. raw jumbo shrimp, peeled and deveined
2 cups flour
½ cup cornstarch
¼ cup cornmeal
½ teaspoon baking powder
½ cup milk
1 egg
3 cups water
2 teaspoons soy sauce, with a little vinegar added

Combine above ingredients, except shrimp, to make thin batter. Toss shrimp in it very lightly, just enough to cover quickly. Fry at 375° for 3 minutes. Drain on absorbent paper and serve immediately with cocktail sauce. Serves 10.

OYSTER BEIGNETS*

1 8-oz. can oysters
¼ cup butter or margarine
1 cup milk
1 cup flour
½ teaspoon sugar
4 eggs

Drain oysters well. Chop. Set aside. Combine butter and milk over low heat until butter is melted. Add flour, to which sugar has been added, all at once to the pot and stir vigorously until mixture forms a ball and leaves sides of pan. Remove from heat. Add eggs one at a time, beating well after each addition until a stiff batter is formed. Add oysters to the batter and mix well. Drop by teaspoonfuls into deep fat at 350°. Fry approximately 3 minutes until browned. Drain on absorbent paper. Serve with cocktail sauce. Serves 12 to 14 as appetizer.

Main Dishes

BUTTERFLY SHRIMP*

1 lb. raw shrimp
2 cups all-purpose flour, sifted
1 teaspoon salt
2 eggs
2 cups ice water
4 tablespoons salad oil

Peel shrimp, leaving tail and last segment of shell intact. Devein. Cut down back of shrimp along center line, but not cutting through. Wash and pat dry. Press to open. Combine remaining ingredients until just blended. Dip shrimp in batter. Fry in deep, hot fat at 375° for about 3 minutes, until golden. Drain on absorbent paper. Serves 6.

STUFFED FRIED SHRIMP*

1 slice boiled sandwich ham
6 water chestnuts
2 scallions
1 sprig parsley
3 tablespoons sesame seeds
1 cup bread crumbs
1 egg
2 lbs. large shrimp, in shell
1 cup cornstarch
2 eggs, beaten
1 cup bread crumbs

In blender, chop very fine and combine ham, water chestnuts, scallions, parsley, and sesame seeds. Mix together with 1 cup bread crumbs and 1 egg. Clean and devein shrimp, leaving tails on. Split shrimp down the back, but not through. Stuff with blended mixture and force back to original shape. Dip shrimp in cornstarch, then in beaten eggs, then in bread crumbs. Fry in deep, hot fat at 375° for about 5 minutes, until golden brown. Drain on absorbent paper and serve hot with soy sauce. Serves 6.

For later use, freeze when cool, placing in shallow pan and covering with aluminum foil. When ready to serve, bake while still frozen in 350° oven for 25 minutes, or fry still frozen shrimp in deep, hot fat at 325° for 2 to 3 minutes, until heated through.

STUFFED FISH FILLETS*

2 lbs. fillet of sole or flounder
2 tablespoons lemon juice
4 tablespoons salad oil
½ cup dry white wine
Salt and pepper to taste
2 tablespoons butter
1½ tablespoons flour
1 cup milk
¼ teaspoon dry mustard
3 tablespoons grated Parmesan cheese
1 cup cooked lobster or shrimp, cut fine
1 cup fine, dry bread crumbs
1 egg, beaten

Cut fillets in serving pieces and marinate in lemon juice, oil, wine, salt, and pepper for at least 1 hour. Meanwhile, in small saucepan, melt butter, stir in flour, and gradually add milk, stirring constantly. When blended and thickened, add dry mustard and Parmesan cheese. Cool slightly and add lobster or shrimp. Allow to cool, place on center of each piece of fillet, roll, and fasten with wooden toothpicks. Roll in bread crumbs, dip in egg and then roll in bread crumbs again. Fry in deep fat at 375°, for about 4 to 5 minutes, or until golden. Drain on absorbent paper and serve with mayonnaise mixed with equal quantity of chili sauce and prepared horseradish. Serves 6.

BUTTERFLY LOBSTER*

6 cooked lobster tails, shelled
6 water chestnuts, sliced
⅔ cup cornstarch
2 eggs
⅓ cup cornstarch

Cut cooked lobster meat into 1-inch sections. Slit each piece in center, and stuff with slice of water chestnut. Fasten with wooden toothpick, if necessary. Make batter of ⅔ cup cornstarch and eggs. Dip lobster in ⅓ cup dry cornstarch, then in batter. Fry at 375° until golden, about 3 minutes. Drain on absorbent paper and serve with Chinese mustard and soy sauce. Serves 8.

FRIED FISH FRITTERS*

2 cups flaked, cooked, boned fish
3 eggs, separated
3 tablespoons flour
½ teaspoon salt
⅛ teaspoon pepper
⅛ teaspoon garlic powder
½ teaspoon onion powder

Beat egg yolks until light; add flour and seasonings and fish. Beat egg whites until stiff and fold into fish mixture. Drop by tablespoon-fuls into hot fat, 360°, and fry until golden. Serves 4.

FRENCH-FRIED EGGPLANT*

2 lbs. eggplant
¾ teaspoon salt
⅛ teaspoon pepper
3 tablespoons flour
1 egg, beaten
½ cup dry bread crumbs

Peel eggplant and cut into 3-inch strips. Sprinkle with salt and pepper and dredge with flour. Dip in beaten egg, then bread crumbs. Deep fry at 375° until golden, about 3 minutes. Drain on absorbent paper. Serve as a main course or side dish. Serves 8.

Other Uses For Deep Fryer

Soups

BOUILLABAISSE

3 tablespoons olive oil
1 large onion, sliced
2 cloves garlic, crushed
2 tomatoes, skinned and sliced
2 teaspoons salt
1 teaspoon pepper
1 bay leaf
½ teaspoon thyme
2 tablespoons freshly chopped parsley
1 quart boiling water
1 cup clam juice
1 1½-lb. lobster, cut into pieces
16 raw shrimp, shelled and deveined
16 mussels, in the shell, scrubbed clean and debearded
1½ lbs. white fish, cod or halibut, deboned and cut into serving pieces
1 cup dry white wine

Place oil and onion in deep fryer and brown at 375° for 5 minutes. Add garlic, tomatoes, salt, pepper, bay leaf, thyme, and parsley and cook 2 minutes more. Lower temperature to 325°, pour in boiling water and clam juice and simmer 15 minutes. Add shellfish, fish, and wine and simmer 15 minutes more. Remove bayleaf. Serves 8.

BARLEY CREAM SOUP*

2 lbs. marrow bones
2 medium onions, sliced
1 small carrot
2 stalks celery
1½ quarts cold water
2 teaspoons salt
½ teaspoon mixed herbs for soup
2 tablespoons pearl barley
1 tablespoon butter
Dash nutmeg
½ pint light sweet cream

Combine bones, onions, carrot, celery, cold water, salt, and herbs in deep fryer and bring to a boil at 400°. Lower temperature to 325° and simmer for 1 hour. Strain, cool and skim surface fat. Reheat liquid at 325°. Add barley, butter, and nutmeg. Simmer for 3 hours, adding cream during last 15 minutes. Serves 6.

NOTE: Freeze in large container. Reheat frozen block in fryer, until hot, about 1 hour at 350°.

Fricassées

RABBIT FRICASSÉE*

3 lbs. rabbit, cut into small joints
1 large onion
8 mushrooms
1 teaspoon salt
¼ teaspoon pepper
1 teaspoon lemon juice
1 teaspoon rosemary
1 clove garlic, minced
2 tablespoons butter
3 tablespoons flour
1 cup milk
1 cup chicken broth

Place rabbit in deep fryer with onion, mushrooms, salt, pepper, lemon juice, rosemary, and garlic. Heat at 400° for 10 minutes, then lower temperature to 325° and simmer for 2½ hours. Remove rabbit to serving platter. In blender, blend gravy. Increase temperature in fryer to 375°, melt butter and stir in flour. Add blended gravy, milk and broth and stir until sauce is thickened. Pour over meat. Serves 4.

NOTE: May be frozen in gravy, and reheated by simmering.

CHICKEN FRICASSÉE*

1 large onion, sliced
3 tablespoons chicken fat
2 lbs. chicken giblets
½ cup chicken broth
1 teaspoon salt
¼ teaspoon pepper
½ teaspoon garlic powder
2 tablespoons chicken fat
1 small onion, blender chopped
1 lb. ground beef
3 tablespoons cold water
3 tablespoons dry bread crumbs or matzo meal
1 egg
1 teaspoon salt
¼ teaspoon pepper
½ teaspoon garlic powder

In deep fryer, sauté sliced onion in chicken fat. Add giblets, broth, and first group of seasonings. Simmer for one hour at 275°. Meanwhile, in skillet, brown chopped onion. Add to ground beef with water, bread crumbs or matzo meal, egg, and seasonings. Roll into balls the size of walnuts. When giblets have been simmering for 1 hour, add meatballs and continue to simmer for another 40 minutes. Serves 6.

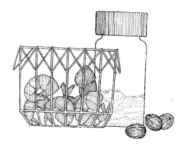

Stews

LAMB AND EGGPLANT STEW*

3 lbs. shoulder lamb, cut into 2-inch cubes
3 tablespoons vegetable fat
1 medium onion, chopped
½ cup tomato paste
1 8-oz. can tomato sauce
1 teaspoon salt
4 peppercorns
½ teaspoon basil
½ teaspoon garlic powder
1 medium eggplant, peeled and cubed
1 green pepper, seeded and diced
4 medium potatoes, pared and diced

In deep fryer, brown lamb in hot fat at 400°. Reduce temperature to 325°, add onion, tomato paste and sauce and seasonings and simmer for 1½ to 2 hours, until meat is tender. Add eggplant and potatoes and cook another 25 minutes. Serves 6.

NOTE: May be frozen when completed or before vegetables have been added. If meat is frozen alone, defrost when ready to serve, heat, add vegetables and proceed as above.

IRISH STEW*

4 tablespoons pearl barley
3 lbs. stewing lamb, cut into 2-inch cubes
4 large onions, sliced
6 medium potatoes, peeled and cubed
1 quart beef broth
1 teaspoon chervil
1½ teaspoons salt
¼ teaspoon pepper
½ teaspoon garlic powder

Rinse barley thoroughly and blanch. Place with meat, onion slices, potatoes, water, and seasoning in deep fryer, potatoes forming top layer. Bring to a quick boil at 425°, then reduce temperature to 325° and simmer for 2 hours. Serves 6.

Roasts

LEMON VEAL ROAST*

3 lbs. boned, rolled veal roast
1½ teaspoons salt
¼ teaspoon pepper
1 bay leaf
4 whole peppercorns
½ teaspoon mace
4 whole allspice
2 whole carrots
2 ribs celery
2 cups chicken broth
⅓ cup butter
½ cup flour
1 egg yolk
2 tablespoons lemon juice
1 lb. egg noodles, cooked according to package directions

Place meat in deep fryer, add seasonings, vegetables, and chicken broth. Cook at 325° for 1½ hours. In saucepan, melt butter, stir in flour, and add stock from the cooked meat. Heat thoroughly. Place in blender, add carrots and celery and blend to a smooth sauce. Just before serving, add egg yolk and lemon juice and blend 1 second. Pour over sliced roast and serve with hot, cooked noodles. Serves 6.

SAUERBRATEN*

3 lbs. beef rump roast
1½ cups wine vinegar
1½ cups water
1 tablespoon salt
1½ tablespoons sugar
1 bay leaf
1 clove garlic
3 whole cloves
1 tablespoon pickling spices
1 large onion, sliced
2 tablespoons cooking oil
1 tablespoon flour
1 lb. broad noodles, cooked according to package directions

In large bowl, marinate meat in mixture of vinegar and water. Add salt, sugar, bay leaf, garlic, cloves, pickling spices, and onion. Cover and refrigerate for 2 or 3 days. In deep fryer, heat oil and brown meat. Add flour into fryer fat, stir until smooth, then add the marinating liquid and spices. Cook at 325° for about 2 hours, until meat is tender. Serve sliced with cooked noodles. Serves 6.

Eight

The Knife Sharpener,
the Electric Knife,
and the Slicing Machine

The Knife Sharpener, the Electric Knife, and the Slicing Machine

This book would not be complete without the acknowledgment that the kitchen knife is the most essential tool of the culinary trade. To be sharpened, it depends, as does its user, on an electrical appliance. True, improvements such as the electric knife and the slicing machine are of great help, and are more justifiably categorized as appliances, but there is many a job only your trusted knife will handle. To guarantee peak performance, your knife sharpener should be on hand and used almost daily, so that you will know the genuine pleasure of maximum efficiency in the use of your knives.

The electric knife and the slicing machine are important variations of slicing appliances. A sharp knife, for some cutting needs, requires the exertion of manual pressure. A slicer will do the job more easily, while the electric knife, requiring a minimum of care and storage space, can perform a variety of shredding, mincing, cubing, and carving chores both in the kitchen and at the table and needs no more than a quick rinsing of its blades when the job is done.

Each of these cutting tools lends its own measure of efficiency. Experience and experimentation will dictate whether the slicer is preferable for preparing paper-thin slices of salami and cheese for appetizers or whether the electric knife is best for cutting through a watermelon. When storage limitations or expense are a consideration, however, you may comfortably meet all your cutting needs with the electric sharpener and an assortment of good kitchen knives.

Appetizers

CHICKEN LIVER CANAPÉS*

1 8-oz. package cream cheese
½ lb. sweet butter
2 cups all-purpose flour, sifted

Allow cream cheese and butter to attain room temperature. Mix with fingers, add flour, knead, and refrigerate until firm, or freeze for future use. When ready to use, roll flat, and cut into 2 x 2-inch squares. Place filling (see p. 292) in center of half the squares, cover with other half, and press edges together with tines of fork, first moistening bottom edges to encourage sticking. Place on ungreased cookie sheet and bake at 350° for 15 to 20 minutes, or until puffy and golden. Serve hot. Makes 30.

FILLING*

5 chicken livers, cut fine with sharp knife
1 teaspoon finely cut onion
6 large mushrooms, cut fine
2 tablespoons butter
1 hard-boiled egg, chopped fine
2 tablespoons broth or gravy

Sauté livers, onion, and mushrooms in butter. When browned, stir in egg and broth and mix well.

NOTE: For other fillings, see chapter 2 under hot canapé fillings.

FILLED FRENCH BREAD

1 long thin loaf of French bread
2 large green peppers, seeded
2 tomatoes, peeled
2 teaspoons salt
4 teaspoons grated onion
4 tablespoons butter
1 lb. cream cheese

Chop seeded green peppers and peeled tomatoes with very sharp knife or electric knife. Drain and mix with other ingredients. Hollow out French bread; fill cavity tightly with mixture. Wrap in aluminum foil and chill overnight. Slice very thinly with a very sharp knife just before serving. Slice only when very cold. Serves 20.

STUFFED CUCUMBERS

¼ cup soft butter
1 cup grated sharp Cheddar cheese
½ lb. bacon, cooked crisp and crumbled
2 tablespoons milk
½ teaspoon garlic powder
¼ teaspoon Worcestershire sauce
1 large cucumber

Combine butter, cheese, bacon, milk, and seasonings, and mash until well blended. Cut cucumber in half lengthwise and scoop out pulp, leaving ½-inch shell. Pack tightly with cheese mixture and chill thoroughly for several hours. Cut halves into ½-inch slices to serve. Serves 8.

CELERY KNOB SALAD

21 celery knobs, boiled until soft
½ cup mayonnaise
2 teaspoons lemon juice
¼ teaspoon garlic salt
1 tablespoon prepared mustard

Pare celery knobs and cut into strips, as thinly as possible. (A very sharp knife is essential.) Combine other ingredients and add to celery strips. Chill to serve. Serve on lettuce leaves. Serves 6.

HERRING SALAD WITH BEETS

1½ lbs. salt herring, boned and trimmed
2 medium potatoes, boiled and peeled
4 medium beets, cooked and peeled
1 large apple, pared
½ Spanish onion
1 tablespoon sugar
2 tablespoons vinegar
¼ teaspoon pepper
½ cup sour cream
2 tablespoons mayonnaise

Soak herring overnight in cold water. Drain and cut herring, potatoes, beets, and apples into small cubes. Finely chop onion and add remaining ingredients, tossing lightly. Chill well. Serves 12 to 14.

DANISH CUCUMBERS

2 large cucumbers
1 teaspoon salt
3 tablespoons sugar
½ cup white vinegar

Peel and slice cucumbers very thinly. Marinate in remaining ingredients overnight. Before serving, drain off liquid and decorate with fresh or dehydrated dill or finely chopped parsley. May be used as appetizer or salad. Serves 10 to 12.

ORIENTAL DIP

1 cup sour cream
1 cup chilled mayonnaise
1 tablespoon soy sauce
Salt to taste
2 cloves garlic, minced
¼ cup chopped onion
¼ cup minced fresh parsley
2 tablespoons chopped candied ginger
¼ cup chopped water chestnuts

Combine sour cream, mayonnaise, soy sauce, and salt. Add garlic, minced through garlic press, then chopped ingredients. Chill and serve with sesame crackers. Serves 10 to 12.

Main Dishes

CHICKEN CURRY*

3 whole chicken breasts, skinned, boned and cut into 1-inch cubes
4 medium onions
2 cloves garlic
4 tablespoons vegetable oil
3 teaspoons curry powder
½ teaspoon salt
1 carrot, grated
½ cup chicken broth

Chop onions and garlic finely, and sauté in oil until golden. Add curry powder and fry a little more. Add the chicken, seasoned with salt, and simmer slowly, covering the saucepan. Do not add any broth yet unless meat sticks to pan, and then very sparingly. When tender, about 35 minutes, stir in carrot to thicken gravy. Cook 10 minutes more; then slowly add broth. Serve with rice and side dishes of peanuts, coconut, raisins, bananas, etc. Serves 6.

TURKEY CASSEROLE*

2 cups diced, cooked turkey
1 cup sliced celery
½ cup water
¼ cup butter
¼ cup flour
1½ cups milk
½ teaspoon salt
⅛ teaspoon pepper
¼ teaspoon poultry seasoning
¼ cup butter
2½ cups bread crumbs (or 5 slices toast, cubed)

Cook celery 5 minutes in water. Drain, reserving liquid. To make sauce, melt ¼ cup butter, stir in flour, combine reserved liquid with the milk, and add to mixture, heating and stirring until thick. Add seasonings. Melt other ¼ cup butter and add to bread crumbs. Butter 2-quart casserole. Place half the bread on bottom, then turkey and celery. Pour sauce over this, then top with rest of bread crumbs and push these in until covered with sauce. Bake 20 to 25 minutes at 350°. Serves 6.

SWEET-AND-PUNGENT DUCKLING*

1 duckling, ready to cook
1 teaspoon salt
¼ teaspoon pepper
1 green pepper
4 slices canned pineapple, cut into 1 inch wedges
2 cups canned pineapple juice
¼ cup sugar
¼ teaspoon garlic salt
¼ cup cider vinegar
4 tablespoons cornstarch
¼ cup water
2 cups rice, steamed

Wash and dry duck. Rub body cavity lightly with salt, and season bird with salt and pepper. Roast in open pan with no water at 325° until thick portion of leg feels soft when pressed and leg moves easily. Allow 2½ hours for 4-pound bird, 2¾ to 3 hours for 5 pounds. If crisper skin is desired, roast at 350° until tender— about 2 to 2½ hours. One half hour before duck is done, use sharp knife to cut green pepper into 1-inch squares and to cut pineapple slices into 1-inch cubes. Place juice, sugar, garlic salt, and vinegar in saucepan and bring to a boil; then add green pepper and pine- apple and bring to a boil again. Blend cornstarch with the ¼ cup of water and add to mixture in saucepan. Cook over low heat until thick (about 5 minutes), stirring constantly. Cut duck into serving pieces, place on serving platter, and pour sauce over bird. Serve with steamed rice. Serves 4 to 5.

NOTE: If duck is to be frozen, cook as above and dismember into serving pieces. Freeze in container until ready to use. Since freezing or refrigeration tends to make the sauce cloudy (although taste is not affected), it is recommended that the sauce be prepared just before serving. To serve, defrost duck pieces and place in flat heat-and-serve casserole or roasting pan and heat through at 350°. Prepare sauce while duck is heating. Pour sauce over heated duck and keep hot in oven at 300° until ready to serve.

BEEF BURGUNDY*

2 lbs. boneless steak (sirloin or chuck)
¼ lb. butter
6 medium onions, sliced
1 beef bouillon cube
½ cup hot water
1 cup Burgundy wine
2 teaspoons salt
¼ teaspoon pepper
⅛ teaspoon thyme
1 tablespoon paprika
1 bay leaf, crumbled
½ lb. mushrooms, sliced
1 tablespoon flour
½ pint sour cream
1 lb. macaroni, cooked according to package directions

With very sharp knife, cut meat into cubes and brown in butter. Add onions and brown. Dissolve bouillon cube in water and add along with wine and seasonings. Cover and simmer for 3 hours. Stir in flour and mushrooms, and simmer another ½ hour, stirring occasionally. Serve with sour cream and cooked macaroni. Serves 6.

NOTE: To freeze, omit sour cream until reheated and ready to serve.

CHINESE STEAK

2 lbs. boneless steak (sirloin or round)
3 tablespoons vegetable oil
2 large onions, sliced thin
1 clove garlic, minced
1 can chicken broth
1 teaspoon salt
¼ teaspoon pepper
2 teaspoons soy sauce
2 green peppers, cut in strips
4 ribs celery, sliced on bias
2 tablespoons cornstarch
½ cup cold water

Cut steak in 2-inch strips. Brown in oil for several minutes. Add onions, garlic, chicken broth, salt, pepper, and soy sauce, cover, and simmer until meat is tender (about 1½ hours). Add green peppers and celery; stir and simmer until vegetables are heated through but still crisp. Add cornstarch mixed with water and simmer 5 minutes, stirring constantly. Serve with hot rice. Serves 6.

OLIVE POT ROAST*

1 3-lb. eye round roast
1 2-oz. bottle stuffed green olives, whole
1 cup chopped onion
2 teaspoons salt
2 tablespoons vegetable oil
½ cup white vinegar
3 cups water

Using a very sharp pointed knife, cut 1-inch slash through the center of entire roast, and stuff it with half the olives and half the onion. Salt meat; then sprinkle vinegar all over it. Using a heavy kettle, sear roast in oil on all sides, add water, remaining olives, and onion. Reduce heat and simmer for three hours, turning occasionally. Allow to cool slightly before slicing with slicer or electric knife. Serve with gravy made from pan drippings. Serves 4 to 6.

BRISKET*

1 5 to 6-lb. beef brisket
½ teaspoon ground ginger
½ teaspoon dry mustard
1 medium onion, sliced
½ cup water
1 teaspoon Worcestershire sauce
½ cup ketchup
1 teaspoon vinegar
1 tablespoon brown sugar

Season brisket with ginger and dry mustard. Bake at 375° for 2¾ hours. Drain off fat. Add sliced onions, water, and Worcestershire sauce mixed with ketchup, pouring over brisket. Add vinegar mixed with brown sugar. Stir in roasting pan and gently baste brisket. Continue baking for 45 minutes more, basting continuously. When done, remove brisket from roasting pan, cool slightly, and slice thinly on the bias. Gravy may be served as is or mixed with 2 tablespoons of flour to thicken it. Serves 8 to 10.

MEATBALLS IN CABBAGE SAUCE*

2 lbs. ground chuck
1 envelope dehydrated onion soup
½ cup ketchup
1 egg
¾ cup fresh bread crumbs
3 tablespoons hot water
3 tablespoons salad oil

Mix all ingredients, adding a little more hot water, if necessary, to reach proper consistency for rolling. Make small meat balls. the size of a walnut. Brown in oil. Drain meatballs on paper towels.

SAUCE

3 tablespoons salad oil
1 head cabbage, shredded
1 large onion, chopped
3 7-oz. cans tomato sauce
1 box white raisins
Juice of 2 lemons
Sugar to taste
Salt and pepper to taste

Brown cabbage and onion in oil. Add remaining ingredients and simmer about 30 to 35 minutes, or until tender. Add meatballs and cook another 15 minutes. Serves 14 to 16 as appetizer, or 8 as a main course.

LARDED VEAL ROAST

1 3-lb. shoulder of veal
½ teaspoon salt
⅛ lb. salt pork
3 tablespoons bacon fat
⅛ lb. boiled ham
½ cup beef broth or water

SAUCE

1 cup sour cream
4 egg yolks
¾ cup grated Parmesan cheese
1 teaspoon cornstarch
2 tablespoons capers
1 tablespoon melted butter
1 tablespoon bread crumbs
1 tablespoon grated Parmesan cheese

Salt meat. Lard with cubes of salt pork and ham by piercing meat with larding needle or sharp knife and inserting cubes of pork and ham. Place meat in deep kettle, brown in bacon fat, add soup stock, and simmer for 1½ hours, turning once or twice. Slice into thin, uniform slices and arrange in ovenproof serving dish. Prepare sauce by beating sour cream, egg yolks, cheese, and cornstarch together in top of double boiler, heating and beating until thick. Add capers. Pour over meat, pour melted butter on top, sprinkle with bread crumbs and cheese. Bake in hot oven 5 to 10 minutes, or until crusty. Serves 4 to 6.

VEAL AND PEPPERS*

2 lbs. veal cutlets, cut into narrow strips 2-inches long
1 large onion, cut in julienne strips
4 green peppers, cut in julienne strips
4 tablespoons vegetable oil
4 tablespoons soy sauce
2 teaspoons cornstarch
⅛ teaspoon pepper
¼ teaspoon monosodium glutamate

Fry julienne strips of onion and green pepper in 2 tablespoons of oil until shiny but not brown. Remove from pan. Place remaining oil, 2 tablespoons soy sauce, and the meat in pan. Sprinkle with cornstarch, and brown. Add green pepper and onion mixture, with remaining 2 tablespoons of soy sauce, pepper, and monosodium glutamate. Simmer, covered, for 25 minutes, or until meat is tender. Serves 6.

SHRIMP STROGANOFF

2 lbs. cooked shrimp, shelled and deveined
2 tablespoons flour
1½ teaspoons salt
¼ teaspoon pepper
¼ teaspoon nutmeg
½ cup finely minced onion
4 tablespoons butter
1 lb. fresh mushrooms, thinly sliced
1 14½-oz. can chicken broth
¼ cup dry white wine
1 cup sour cream
A few sprigs parsley, chopped

Cut shrimp into narrow crescents, reserving a few for garnish. Dust with flour and seasonings and sauté with minced onion in butter until golden. Add mushrooms and flour remaining after dusting. Blend. Add chicken broth and simmer 20 minutes. Add wine, stirring until well combined. Simmer just until heated through. Remove from heat. Add sour cream, stir, and garnish with reserved shrimp and parsley. Serves 4.

SEAFOOD CASSEROLE*

1½ cups long grain rice
1 lb. wild rice
2 lbs. cleaned, raw shrimp
2 quarts water
2 tablespoons vinegar
2 cans crab meat
1 can pimiento strips
3 cans cream of mushroom soup
2 tablespoons butter
1 lb. fresh mushrooms, sliced
1 green pepper, diced
2 onions, diced
1 teaspoon salt
½ lb. almonds, sliced and browned in 325° oven for 15 minutes

Cook white rice according to package directions. Wash and cook wild rice. Combine the two kinds of rice in deep casserole. Cool. In water to which vinegar has been added, boil shrimp for 5 minutes; set aside. Combine crab meat, pimiento, and soup; stir into rice in casserole. Sauté in butter the mushrooms, green pepper, and onions, season with salt, and add to rice mixture. Bake at 350° for 1 hour, placing shrimp in casserole for the last 5 to 10 minutes of cooking time. Sprinkle with roasted almonds before serving. Serves 10 to 12.

NOTE: To freeze, proceed as above, but do not bake or add shrimp or almonds. Store in covered casserole. Keep the uncooked shrimp frozen, and freeze toasted almonds in small container. When ready to serve, heat rice mixture through thoroughly; meanwhile, boil the shrimp, and add at end of cooking period. Top casserole with frozen almonds at this time also so they will be heated.

Buffet Platters

COLD MEAT LOAF*

2 lbs. ground beef
1 teaspoon salt
¼ teaspoon pepper
1 large onion, minced fine (in blender, preferably)
1 carrot, blender grated
2 eggs, separated
1 cup corn flakes
1 cup cold milk
2 tablespoons butter, softened
2 tablespoons fresh dill, chopped

Mix all ingredients except egg whites. Place in 10 x 5½ x 2½-inch loaf pan. Beat egg whites until stiff, and spread over meat to ice top of the loaf. Bake at 350° for 1 hour. Chill, unmold, and slice with sharp knife when very cold. Serves 6 to 8.

GLAZED HAM WITH CRANBERRY SAUCE*

1 3-lb. canned ham
1 cup currant jelly
2 teaspoons dry mustard

Melt currant jelly over low flame until liquid, about 8 to 10 minutes. Mix jelly with dry mustard and spread on ham. Bake according to directions on can. Slice with very sharp knife or on slicer when cold, and serve with cranberry sauce. Serves 12.

CRANBERRY SAUCE

1 can jellied cranberry sauce
¼ teaspoon cloves
⅛ teaspoon cinnamon
2 tablespoons ruby port wine

In blender, blend all ingredients together until smooth.

PICKLED TONGUE WITH HORSERADISH SAUCE*

1 3 to 4 lb. fresh beef tongue
4 tablespoons vinegar in 2 quarts of water
1 lemon, sliced
1 clove garlic, sliced
2 onions, sliced
6 whole cloves
6 peppercorns
2 tablespoons mixed pickling spices
2 teaspoons salt
¼ teaspoon sour salt
1 teaspoon sugar
Pinch of alum
1 cup sour cream
3 tablespoons prepared white horseradish

Cover tongue with vinegar and water. Add lemon, garlic, onions, and all seasonings. Cover, and let stand at room temperature for a day. Then, refrigerate for at least 2 days or longer, if possible. (Up to 2 weeks is permissible.) To cook, remove lemon slices and simmer, covered, about 2½ to 3 hours (allow 45 to 55 minutes per lb.), until tongue is tender. Cool in broth about 2 hours, and peel skin while tongue is still warm. Then immerse in clear cold water, and let stand for 1 hour, changing water frequently to keep it cold as this will seal the juices in the meat. Refrigerate until ready to serve. Slice very thinly on the bias, starting at the tip, adjusting the angle so the slices are constantly on the bias. Serve with horseradish sauce, prepared by mixing sour cream with white horseradish. Sauce should not be frozen. Serves 8 to 10.

Side Dishes

CRANBERRY MOLD

2 cups fresh cranberries
1¼ cups water
1 cup sugar
1 package cherry gelatin dessert
1 cup diced celery
½ cup diced apple
½ cup chopped nuts
¼ teaspoon salt

Cook cranberries in water until soft, about 10 minutes. Add sugar and cook an additional 5 minutes. Pour boiling mixture over gelatin dessert, stir until dissolved, then chill. When practically set, add chopped ingredients and salt. Pour into ring mold, chill until firm. Turn out on platter. Serves 8 to 10.

CELERY ORIENTAL

3 cups celery, cut in diagonal slices
1 teaspoon salt
1 cup water
1 cup fresh mushrooms, sliced
3 tablespoons butter
¼ cup toasted slivered almonds
Salt to taste

Add celery slices to boiling salted water. Cook for approximately 5 minutes, so that celery is still crisp. Sauté mushrooms in butter, add celery and almonds, and toss to heat through. Salt to season. Serves 4 to 6.

CRISP-COOKED ASPARAGUS

3 lbs. fresh asparagus
2 cups water
1 teaspoon salt
¼ lb. butter, melted
Juice of 1 lemon

Clean asparagus, discarding tough ends. Slice stalks into 1-inch pieces, cutting on a sharp diagonal angle. Cook covered in rapidly boiling salted water for 3 minutes, so that asparagus is still crisp, and removing from flame before vegetable begins to lose color. Drain. Combine butter and lemon juice and pour over asparagus. Serve immediately. Serves 6 to 8.

GREEN VEGETABLE MEDLEY

¼ lb. butter
2 large onions, sliced thin
1 lb. mushrooms, sliced
3 green peppers, cleaned out and cut into 2-inch strips
8 large outside celery ribs, cut on the diagonal into 2-inch pieces
3 zucchini, unpeeled and thinly sliced
½ teaspoon garlic powder
1 teaspoon salt
¼ teaspoon pepper

Melt butter in heavy skillet, sauté onions until glossy, add remaining vegetables and seasoning, and sauté, stirring very frequently. Cook only until vegetables are glossy, removing from flame while still firm and fresh in color. Serve immediately to 4 to 6.

SQUASH IN SOUR CREAM

1 teaspoon salt
4 cups yellow squash
2 cups water
Dash pepper
1 medium onion, sliced
2 tablespoons butter
1 cup sour cream
¼ teaspoon salt
1 teaspoon fresh dill, finely chopped

Covered, simmer squash in salted water just until tender, about 15 minutes. Drain well and add pepper. Sauté onion in butter just till it is shiny but not brown, remove from heat, and add sour cream and salt. Place squash in serving dish, pour cream mixture over it, and sprinkle with dill. Serves 4 to 6.

CHEESED ZUCCHINI*

6 zucchini, unpeeled
1 teaspoon salt
¼ teaspoon garlic powder
⅛ teaspoon oregano
⅛ teaspoon pepper
3 tomatoes
Salt, pepper, and oregano, as above
2 medium onions
4 slices sharp processed American cheese
6 strips bacon, uncooked

With sharp knife, quarter zucchini lengthwise. Place in bottom of 9 x 13-inch baking dish. Sprinkle with some of the salt, garlic powder, oregano, and pepper. Slice tomatoes and place over squash. Season as zucchini. Slice onions, and place in layer over tomatoes. Cover with cheese slices, and top with a layer of bacon. Bake uncovered in 350° oven for 45 minutes. Serves 6.

CHEESED ONION BAKE*

6 medium onions, thinly sliced
¼ cup butter
3 tablespoons flour
2 cups milk
1 teaspoon salt
Dash pepper
½ lb. processed American cheese

Slice onions and place in deep casserole. In saucepan, melt butter, add flour, and gradually add milk, stirring and cooking until thick. Stir in seasonings and cheese, mixing until well blended. Pour over onions and bake at 350° for 1 hour. Serves 6.

NOTE: Thinly sliced raw potatoes or a combination of onions and potatoes may be used instead of onions alone, with the rest of the recipe remaining the same.

GLAZED CARROTS*

2 bunches carrots
1 cup honey
1 tablespoon butter

Pare carrots and slice. Boil in salted water until tender but still firm. Drain and place in shallow pan. In saucepan, heat honey and butter together. Pour over carrots and bake at 350° until glaze is set, about 30 minutes. Serves 4 to 6.

CORN PATTIES*

3 ears of fresh corn
¼ cup vegetable oil
6 eggs
2 tablespoons cake flour
1 teaspoon salt
⅛ teaspoon pepper
2 teaspoons grated cheddar cheese

Run the point of sharp knife down the middle of each row of corn kernels lengthwise, splitting them down the middle. With the dull side of knife blade, press kernels off cob, scraping remainder off with a spoon. Beat eggs; add flour, seasonings, cheese, and cut corn. Heat oil in electric skillet, and drop mixture from spoon, using about 3 tablespoons of batter to form each patty. Flatten to spread batter; turn to cook other side when edges look dry. Serve with applesauce or sour cream. Serves 6.

CUCUMBERS IN SOUR CREAM

3 cucumbers, chilled
1 tablespoon lemon juice
1 teaspoon salt
¼ teaspoon pepper
2 tablespoons chopped chives
1 cup sour cream

Pare and slice cucumbers very thinly. Mix remaining ingredients and pour over cucumbers. Serve chilled. Serves 6.

CABBAGE SALAD

1 head green cabbage, knife shredded
1 head red cabbage, knife shredded
1 large onion, minced (or 2 medium red onions, sliced thinly)
½ cup capers, drained
1 1-lb. can pitted black olives
6 tablespoons salad oil
4 tablespoons wine vinegar
1 teaspoon salt
½ teaspoon garlic powder
¼ teaspoon pepper

Toss cabbage, onion, and capers with remaining ingredients. (More dressing may be needed, depending on size of cabbage heads. Salad should be well covered with dressing, but not wet.) Chill at least 3 hours, longer if possible. Drain before serving. Serves 12 or more.

SALADE PROVENÇAL

6 firm ripe tomatoes
6 green peppers
8 to 10 scallions
½ cup chopped chives
2 small cans flat fillets of anchovies with oil
3 tablespoons salad oil
3 tablespoons wine vinegar
¼ teaspoon garlic powder
¼ teaspoon pepper

Cut each tomato into 8 wedges. Cut green peppers into 2-inch squares. Slice scallions thinly. Toss in chives. Cut each anchovy fillet into 3 sections. Combine these with remaining ingredients. Chill for at least 1 hour, and drain before serving. Serves 6.

WALDORF SALAD

2 cups seedless green grapes, halved
2 cups canned pineapple chunks, drained
2 cups diced, peeled apples
1 cup walnut pieces
1 cup mayonnaise
1 cup heavy cream, whipped

Combine all ingredients and chill. Serves 10 to 12.

CHEF'S SALAD

½ head iceberg lettuce
½ head romaine lettuce
½ head escarole chicory
½ cucumber, unpeeled
2 tomatoes
2 scallions
3 hard-boiled eggs
6 strips bacon, cooked until crisp
3 slices Swiss cheese
3 slices boiled ham
3 slices hard salami

DRESSING

3 tablespoons wine vinegar
5 tablespoons salad oil
Salt and pepper to taste

Tear washed lettuce greens into bite-sized pieces. Dry thoroughly on paper towels and place in salad bowl. Slice cucumber, cut tomatoes into wedges, slice scallions. Cut eggs into wedges, crumble bacon, and cut cheese, ham, and salami into thin strips. Reserve some of the ham and cheese strips to decorate top of salad. Toss greens and combine with remaining ingredients, except egg wedges. Add dressing; toss well, decorate with egg. Serves 8 to 10.

WARM CABBAGE RELISH*

6 strips sliced bacon
1 2-lb. head green cabbage
2 teaspoons salt
1 tablespoon chopped onion
½ teaspoon caraway seeds
2 tablespoons cider vinegar
⅛ teaspoon pepper

Fry bacon in large skillet and remove when crisp, reserving fat. With sharp knife, shred cabbage. Add salt, and let stand. Sauté onion in bacon fat, add caraway seeds, vinegar, pepper, and cabbage. Toss lightly. Sprinkle with crumbled bacon. Serve warm. Serves 8.

Desserts

SHERRIED FRUIT

6 fresh peaches
1 cup fresh strawberries
1 fresh pineapple
2 cups sweet sherry

Pour boiling water over peaches, then remove skins. Cut into thin wedges, cutting from outside toward pit, across the whole peach, maintaining the same angle as you go around for even, attractive slices. Cut strawberries in half. Pare pineapple by standing fruit up and cutting from the top down. (Here the electric knife is invaluable!) Remove eyes. Slice pineapple and cut into chunks. Combine all fruits and soak in sherry for several hours, keeping refrigerated. Serves 8 to 10.

DUTCH APPLE CAKE*

2½ cups flour, sifted
2 teaspoons double-acting baking powder
2 tablespoons sugar
1 cup butter
1 teaspoon vanilla
1 egg, slightly beaten
8 green cooking apples
1 cup heavy cream, whipped (optional)

TOPPING

1½ cups sugar
2½ tablespoons flour
½ teaspoon salt
¼ cup butter
1 teaspoon cinnamon

Sift the flour and baking powder together. Add sugar; then cut in butter until the mixture is crumbly. Add vanilla to the slightly beaten egg, and blend with flour mixture. Press evenly into bottom and sides of 18 x 12 x 1-inch pan. Prepare cinnamon crumb topping by combining all topping ingredients. Pare, quarter, and core apples, and with very sharp knife, slice each quarter into the thinnest possible wedges, placing them on pastry dough in rows and overlapping the slices until all the dough is covered. Sprinkle topping over apples. Bake at 350° for 45 minutes. Cool, cut into serving pieces, and serve with whipped cream, if desired. Serves 12 to 14.

FILLED ORANGE SHELLS

3 large seedless oranges
1 banana, sliced
½ cup strawberries
¼ cup walnut pieces

SAUCE

3 oz. cream cheese
⅓ cup lime juice
1 tablespoon sugar
1 tablespoon grated orange rind
6 sprigs fresh mint

Cut oranges in half and cut out orange sections, separating each segment from membrane. Discard membranes. To orange sections, add sliced banana, strawberries, which have been halved, and nuts. Heap mixture into orange skins. Beat cream cheese and lime juice with sugar and orange rind until fluffy. Pour over fruit in shells, and decorate with fresh mint. Serves 6.

APPLE CRISP*

6 medium green cooking apples
¼ lb. butter
1 teaspoon cinnamon
½ cup brown sugar
½ cup white sugar
½ cup flour

Pare, core, and slice apples not too thinly. Blend butter, cinnamon, and sugars, then add flour to form crumbly mixture. Add apples, and place mixture in buttered 8 x 8 x 2-inch baking dish. Cover and bake at 350° for 1 hour. Serves 6.

DARK FRUIT CAKE*

3 7¼-oz. packages of pitted dates
1 lb. candied pineapple
1 lb. whole candied red cherries
2 cups all-purpose flour, sifted
2 teaspoons double-acting baking powder
½ teaspoon salt
4 eggs
1 cup granulated sugar
2 lbs. pecan halves

Cut dates and candied pineapple into coarse pieces. Add cherries. Sift, then measure flour, and sift with baking powder and salt onto fruit. Mix well with fingers to assure even coverage of all pieces. Beat eggs until frothy with electric beater. Gradually add sugar, continuing to beat until blended. Add to fruit mixture and mix well. Add nuts, and mix until evenly distributed. Grease two 10 x 5½ x 2½-inch loaf pans, line them with brown paper cut to fit, and grease paper. Pack batter into pans, pressing down to eliminate air spaces. Bake 1½ hours at 275°, or until tops look dry. Let cool 5 minutes, then turn out and remove brown paper. Cool cakes completely before slicing. Use a very sharp knife to cut. Serves 14 to 16.

NOTE: This cake may be kept several weeks. Frozen, it keeps for months.

WHITE FRUIT CAKE*

5 tablespoons rum
1 lb. mixed candied fruit
6 eggs, separated
1 cup sugar
½ lb. butter
2 cups flour
½ lb. raisins
½ cup walnuts

Pour rum over candied fruit and let stand. With electric mixer, beat egg yolks and sugar until lemon colored, add butter, and beat well. Fold in flour, raisins, walnuts, and candied fruit. Beat egg whites until stiff but not dry. Fold into batter. Line two 10 x 5½ x 2½-inch pans with aluminum foil, pour in batter, and bake at 350° for 1½ hours. Serves 12 to 14.

NOTE: This cake, wrapped in aluminum foil, may be kept several weeks. Frozen, it keeps for months.

ORANGE MARMALADE

1½ cups thinly sliced orange slices with rinds
½ cup thinly sliced lemon slices with rinds
1 quart water
Sugar to taste (2 to 3 cups)
1 box powdered pectin

Simmer orange and lemon slices, covered, in water until tender (about 1 hour). Mixture should not cook down to less than 3 cups. If it does, add enough water to measure 3 cups. Add pectin, simmer gently for a few minutes, then add sugar and simmer another ½ hour. Store in sterilized jars, and seal with melted paraffin for long storage. Makes 2 pints marmalade.

NOTE: This marmalade will set slowly. Do not be concerned if it appears thin—allow 2 weeks before using.

Index

39